Unless otherwise stated all Scripture quotations are taken from
the King James Version of the bible (KJV).
New King James Version (NKJV), Modern King James Version
(MKJV), New International Version (NIV), New Living Translation
(NLT), Message Bible (MSG), Amplified Bible (AMP), Bible In Basic
English (BBE), Complete Apostle's Bible (CAB),Good News Bible
(GNB), God's Word Bible (GW), Complete Jewish Bible (CJB)
New International Readers Version (NIRV)

Strong's Hebrew & Greek Dictionaries

(Bold & Italic texts are for emphasis by the author)

ISBN 978-1-77924-268-6

Forty Days On Hope 1st Edition 2023
ISBN NUMBER; 978-1-77924-268-6
EAN NUMBER; 9781779242686
Web; https://www.facebook.com/FortyDaysOnHope

For additional information contact the publisher

Email; thewordoftruthpublications@gmail.com
Web; https://thewordoftruthjc.blogspot.com
https://www.facebook.com/TheWordOfTruthJC
https://www.instagram.com/TheWordOfTruthJC
https://twitter.com/TheWordOf_Truth@TheWordOf_Truth
https://www.youtube.com/@thewordoftruthjasonpaulpullen

Contact the Author

Email; jaycep@hotmail.com
Other Writings by the Author Now That You Are Saved, New
Believers' Foundation, Forty Days On Salvation, Forty days On
Grace, Forty days on Mercy, Forty Days on Righteousness, Forty
Days on Faith, The Word Of Truth Devotions
Web; https://www.facebook.com/NowThatYouRSaved
Web; https://www.facebook.com/NewBelieversFoundation
Web; https://www.facebook.com/FortyDaysOnSalvation
Web; https://www.facebook.com/FortyDaysOnGrace
Web; https://www.facebook.com/FortyDaysOnMercy
Web; https://www.facebook.com/FortyDaysOnRighteousness
Web; https://www.facebook.com/FortyDaysOnFaith

Cover design by

Real Deal Graphic Designs
Email; realdealgraphicdesigns@gmail.com

FORTY DAYS
ON
HOPE

By

Jason Pullen

Hope is an anchor and a divine
connection to great expectations
for the Future.

Book #6 from the series 40 Days with God by Jason Pullen

CONTENTS

Heading	Page

Dedication

- This book is dedicated to the Lord Jesus Christ and His Kingdom. For counting me faithful and by His Power making my hand the pen of a ready writer I thank you Jesus!
- To the Beloved children of God and citizens of His Kingdom. Who stand by the promises of God. Here you will receive full assurance that your trust is not in vain.
- To those who have faced disappointment in life, whether it is a broken heart, a lost dream, a loved one passing away. Be restored with vigour strength and a reason to live with great expectancy
- To those who may have thought of giving up in a situation, a marriage, a sickness, a business or any other a trial. There is reason to still Hope.
- To those who have given up on life and who may even have had suicidal thoughts. This book will cast out all darkness and bring a new dawn to you.

Acknowledgements

I would like to acknowledge the Holy Spirit for reigniting the passion in me to Hope for greater things. As I've written this book I have seen restoration in a lot of areas of my life. Thanks to the Lord Jesus for His Grace that enabled me to put this book together.

I would like to acknowledge Prophet William Undi and everyone at The Beloved Church for their continual prayers and support.

I would like to acknowledge my immediate family who always support everything I do in the Kingdom of God.

Salvation Prayer

Lord Jesus come into my life and be the Lord of my life. I believe that you died for me and rose from the dead. I receive forgiveness for all my sins. I declare that I am saved I am born again. I am filled with the Holy Spirit and washed in the blood of Jesus. In Jesus name. Amen

If you have just prayed this prayer congratulations now starts the beginning of your life in Christ. As we go through these forty days we will get deeper in understanding what you now have access to having received Salvation in Jesus Christ.

FORTY DAYS ON HOPE

INTRODUCTION

Welcome reader to this forty day devotion on Hope. This is part in a series of daily devotions by the author Jason Pullen. Take your time to meditate on the verses, devotions and say out the confessions or prayers to enjoy the full experience from these devotions.

Let's pause and think on the scripture below:

Daniel answered and said, Blessed be the name of God for ever and ever: for wisdom and might are his: And he changeth the times and the seasons: he removeth kings, and setteth up kings: he giveth wisdom unto the wise, and knowledge to them that know understanding: He revealeth the deep and secret things: he knoweth what *is* in the darkness, and the light dwelleth with him. (Dan 2:20-22 KJV)

Praise the Lord! Everything has a time, season and purpose. God reveals things as He desires, all wisdom and knowledge comes from Him. Daniel was shown the Kings dream with the interpretation and this saved him and his peers. There is Power when God reveals secrets. These devotions will bring revelation knowledge, understanding and transforming power to your life.

All numbers, names, dates, events have significance with the Lord Jesus. The number forty has a divine purpose. This is why as instructed by the Holy Spirit I have compiled this forty day series.

We first see with Noah the rain fell for forty days and forty nights (see Gen 7). Moses encountered God on the Mount for forty days and forty nights (see Ex 24). Jesus was led by the Spirit to be tried of satan for forty days and forty nights (see Mat 4). Elijah journeyed on the strength of divine food for forty days and forty nights (see 1 Ki 19). Forty years the children of Israel wandered in the wilderness (see Det 2). At forty years old Moses slew the Egyptian and fled Egypt (see Act 7). Ezekiel prophesied that Egypt would be desolate forty years (Eze 29). All these and more important events match with the number forty.

The number forty can be seen as a time of testing, trial, judgment, transformation, testimony, victory, peace, promise, ending, new beginning and fulfillment. The Holy Spirit revealed to me that forty days is a time of intimacy, rest and transformation leading to the fulfillment of His purpose. Our obedience to His transforming instruction in forty days can result in our victory after forty days. Our disobedience to the Lords instruction can result in a delay of our full victory by forty years. Let us consider the scripture below;

You will die and your corpses will be scattered across this wilderness. Because you have complained against me, none of you over twenty years of age will enter that land. (Num 14:29 GNB)

You will suffer the consequences of your sin for forty years, one year for each of the forty days you spent exploring the land. You will know what it means to have me against you! (Num 14:34 GNB)

Of all the spies who went to spy out the Promised Land only Joshua and Caleb gave a good report. The rest gave a bad report and complained they were also supported by the Israelites. As a result God said for every day spent spying the land, it shall be a year they shall spend wandering the desert. They also would not enter the Promised Land except for Joshua and Caleb. This was later fulfilled.

We can see the children of Israel were right at the doorstep of their promise after a forty day period they could have inherited their promise. Their disobedience and unbelief caused them to miss their promise and delay it's fulfillment by forty years!

Please understand this is not a formula that if you are disobedient your promise will be delayed by forty years but an example of a possibility.

Alternatively we see Jesus Christ who was led by the Holy Spirit soon after His public baptism into the desert for forty days and forty nights. He overcame the testing and temptation this led to the beginning of His ministry.

And there came a voice from heaven, *saying,* Thou art my beloved Son, in whom I am well pleased. And immediately the Spirit driveth him into the wilderness. And he was there in the wilderness forty days, tempted of Satan; and was with the wild beasts; and the angels ministered unto him. Now after that John was put in prison, Jesus came into Galilee, preaching the gospel of the kingdom of God,
(Mar 1:11-14 KJV)

Here we see Jesus coming out from a forty day period to inherit His destiny as opposed to the disobedient children of Israel who delayed their destiny.

Let me emphasize that it does not take God forty days or forty years to fulfill His promises to you. This is not a fixed doctrine or formula for a breakthrough. Jesus Christ can do anything anytime. We must however acknowledge the significance and power forty days with the Lord has. As we have briefly seen many major events in the bible involved the number forty. This is not a law nor is it an Old Testament doctrine.

After his suffering, he showed himself to these men and gave many convincing proofs that he was alive. He appeared to them over a period of forty days and spoke about the kingdom of God.
(Act 1:3 NIV)

Even in the New Testament as shown above forty days carries importance, for after Jesus rose from the dead He showed Himself for forty days before His ascension. These forty day devotions bring the life changing revelation of the specific topic by the Holy Ghost our teacher. Be blessed, encounter the Holy Spirit be transformed, rest, overcome and get your victory in Jesus name.

Jesus Christ the same yesterday, and to day, and for ever. (Heb 13:8 KJV)

HOPE EXPLAINED

Hope is the second of three key virtues in Christianity, the first being Faith the third Love. These three powerful virtues hold the Saints of God. In book five of this series we thoroughly dealt on Faith. Now we will explore the depths of Hope.

And now abide faith, hope, love, these three; but the greatest of these is love. (1Co 13:13 NKJV)

Hope is the Power that binds us to the Promises of God. It locks us fully to the Word of God. It is what makes it impossible for a child of God to give up. So what exactly is Hope? Let's look at Hebrew and Greek words often translated in the bible as hope.

H3176

יָחַל

yâchal

yaw-chal'

A primitive root; to *wait*; by implication to *be patient*, *hope:* - (cause to, have, make to) hope, be pained, stay, tarry, trust, wait.

Re: Strong's dictionary

This is the first of the Hebrew words translated as Hope in the King James Bible. Below is the second most translated

---

Hebrew word as Hope.

H8615

תִּקְוָה

tiqvâh

tik-vaw'

From H6960; literally a *cord* (as an *attachment* (compare H6961)); figuratively *expectancy: -* expectation ([-ted]), hope, live, thing that I long for.

Re: Strong's dictionary

These words are almost the same below are the common Greek words translated as Hope in the English Bible.

G1680

ἐλπίς

elpis

el-pece'

From ἔλπω elpō which is a primary word (to *anticipate*, usually with pleasure); *expectation* (abstract or concrete) or *confidence: -* faith, hope.

Re: Strong's dictionary

G1679

ἐλπίζω

elpizō

el-pid'-zo

From G1680; to *expect* or *confide:* - (have, thing) hope (-d) (for), trust.

Re: Strong's dictionary

We can see that these four words all have something to do with an expectation. An expectation involves expecting; that means waiting for something. The second most translated Hebrew word says that hope is a chord. Praise the Lord. As we get further in this book we will unravel more on this. Below is Hope defined in English.

The feeling that what is wanted can be had or that events will turn out for the best.

To look forward to with desire and reasonable confidence.

Re: Dictionary.com

Hope is the power of God that keeps us attached to His Word and promises. Hope is an anchor to the soul. By Hope we are eternally hooked on the promises of God. It is that unbreakable link that keeps us on track to the fulfilment of the Word of God.

That by two immutable things, in which *it was* impossible for God to lie, we might have a strong

consolation, who have fled for refuge to lay hold upon the hope set before us: Which *hope* we have as an anchor of the soul, both sure and stedfast, and which entereth into that within the veil; (Heb 6:18-19 KJV)

Hope is for the future. The Hope the Lord has given us is what keeps Saints certain of a positive outcome in all things. Hope is our eternal unbreakable bond to the fulfilment of God's Word and Promises. It is a connection that maintains Trust in the destiny the Lord Jesus has set out.

Hope is the power of God that keeps us attached to His Word and promises.

Hope is our eternal unbreakable bond to the fulfilment of God's Word and Promises.

Hope For The Future – Day 1

For I know the plans I have for you," declares the LORD, "plans to prosper you and not to harm you, plans to give you hope and a future. Then you will call upon me and come and pray to me, and I will listen to you. You will seek me and find me when you seek me with all your heart. (Jer 29:11-13 NIV)

As a born again believer in Jesus Christ one thing is certain; that your future is bright. A second thing guaranteed is that your future is brighter and better than your past. Glory to God! He said He has plans to give you a Hope and a future. The life of a Christian always gets better because God is at work. Hope in God is that, better is coming. It is not just better from a bad past but better from a good past too! We grow brighter and better unto perfection.

But the path of the just is like the shining sun, That shines ever brighter unto the perfect day.
(Pro 4:18 NKJV)

The purpose of Hope is for what is yet to come. The Lord says He has good plans for us. We can only plan for what is ahead not what is past. We learn from the past but have high expectation that we will experience a glorious future. Our heavenly Father perfects and makes things beautiful. From the time of creation everything got better as He kept creating things. He waited until everything was prepared and then formed man and put him on the earth. God had Hope for creation in His master plan, with man as the biggest beneficiary,

And God made the beast of the earth according to its kind, cattle according to its kind, and everything that creeps on the earth according to its kind. And God saw that it was good. Then God said, "Let Us make man in Our image, according to Our likeness; let them have dominion over the fish of the sea, over the birds of the air, and over the cattle, over all the earth and over every creeping thing that creeps on the earth." (Gen 1:25-26 NKJV)

From creation we learn that God always brings something better with time. Man was the last to be put on the earth. So there is always a reason to believe your future will be better. The Lord always looks ahead with a promise of something better. Abraham, Isaac and Jacob all held unto the promise of the Lord. They had a word that something good was coming. This kept them going; there was something to live for. Hope maintains your reason for living. There is a promise to be attained.

Our hope and Trust in the Lord links us to the promises of God. We use Faith to receive immediately from the Lord Jesus but Hope enables us to wait. Hope waits with great anticipation to receive what God said. We have a strong reason to look ahead in life because God said He has good plans for us.

Declaration

I declare that my future is brighter because the Lord Jesus has planned my future. I am expecting good things in my life. My life will continually improve in Jesus name.
Amen

Hope in God is that, better is coming. It is not just better from a bad past but better from a good past too!

Hope In God ~ Day 2

"The LORD is my portion," says my soul, "Therefore I hope in Him!" (Lam 3:24 NKJV)

Hope is someone's expectation and anticipation of something good. We can have Hope in different things, people, projects, organizations and so on. All these can fail. It is foolish for someone to pin their Hopes on such, as they can lead to disappointment,

Thus says the LORD: "Cursed is the man who trusts in man And makes flesh his strength, Whose heart departs from the LORD. For he shall be like a shrub in the desert, And shall not see when good comes, But shall inhabit the parched places in the wilderness, In a salt land which is not inhabited. (Jer 17:5-6 NKJV)

Anyone who leans towards man and his systems or anything other than the Lord Jesus Christ, sets them self up for failure. Our Hope must be in the Lord. With Him there is faithfulness. God cannot lie, is faithful and can be trusted. He does not disappoint and send an apology letter or disappear. He remains true and will always be there for a believer to lean on and expect goodness at the end of every situation.

"Blessed is the man who trusts in the LORD, And whose hope is the LORD. For he shall be like a tree planted by the waters, Which spreads out its roots by the river, And will not fear when heat comes; But its leaf will be green, And will not be anxious in the year of drought, Nor will cease from yielding fruit.
(Jer 17:7-8 NKJV)

This is the guarantee for putting your Hope in the Lord. His policy has no expiry date and promises love, joy and peace. Hope in God does not come with any terms and conditions in case of failure. The only terms and conditions are to hear and keep His Word. When you do this you will not be let down. In life certain things require our expectation and Hope in people and institutions but ultimately let your Hope be in God. Do not put your trust and expectation in anything above God.

"Therefore whoever hears these sayings of Mine, and does them, I will liken him to a wise man who built his house on the rock: "and the rain descended, the floods came, and the winds blew and beat on that house; and it did not fall, for it was founded on the rock. "But everyone who hears these sayings of Mine, and does not do them, will be like a foolish man who built his house on the sand: "and the rain descended, the floods came, and the winds blew and beat on that house; and it fell. And great was its fall."
(Mat 7:24-27 NKJV)

We have a faithful God. Put your Hope in Him. Hope in God and His Word is like building your life on a solid foundation. Any other foundation is likened to sand and cannot be trusted. Hope in God gives you a bright and flourishing future against all odds. Just like a tree that is planted by the riverside.

Act

Put all your Hope in God.

Anyone who leans towards man and his systems or anything other than the Lord Jesus Christ, sets them self up for failure.

False Hope – Day 3

Let him not put his hope in what is false, falling into error: for he will get deceit as his reward. His branch is cut off before its time, and his leaf is no longer green.
(Job 15:31-32 BBE)

Truth and lies are two opposing forces like light and darkness. Hope has an opposite which is hopelessness. A hopeless situation is one where there is no faith of anything good coming out of it. False hope on the other hand is deceit; that makes one believe there is a possibility of something good. Whereas there is nothing good that will come. False hope is not Hope at all it is just as good as an empty promise,

Whoso boasteth himself of a false gift *is like* clouds and wind without rain. (Pro 25:14 KJV)

Clouds and winds have a promise of rain, so if there is no rain as a result it's like a false promise. Hope is Hope, with God there is no such thing as false hope. There is no lie or deceit with the Lord, He sticks to His promises. Have full confidence when you trust God that there is no darkness or deceit in what He tells you. God keeps His Word and keeps His promises.

That by two immutable things, in which it is impossible for God to lie, we might have strong consolation, who have fled for refuge to lay hold of the hope set before us.
(Heb 6:18 NKJV)

In the Old Testament there were prophets who prophesied falsely. They gave the people lies to rust in. That was false hope and caused the children of Israel to suffer.

"Behold, you trust in lying words that cannot profit. "Will you steal, murder, commit adultery, swear falsely, burn incense to Baal, and walk after other gods whom you do not know, "and then come and stand before Me in this house which is called by My name, and say, 'We are delivered to do all these abominations'? (Jer 7:8-10 NKJV)

The Lord was correcting the children of Israel; that they could not do wrong things and expect peace. The prophets gave them false hope by saying they were free even though they did wicked things. This is why as a child of God your Hope must be based on the true Word of God. Do not be a fool tossed to and fro by what anyone says even if they are called by God. What they say must agree with the Holy Spirit and His Word. If it is based on a lie it is false and should not be trusted.

"Behold, I am against the prophets," says the LORD, "who use their tongues and say, 'He says.' "Behold, I am against those who prophesy false dreams," says the LORD, "and tell them, and cause My people to err by their lies and by their recklessness. Yet I did not send them or command them; therefore they shall not profit this people at all," says the LORD.
(Jer 23:31-32 NKJV)

It is unfortunate but true that some people use the name

of the Lord falsely to deceive and take advantage of the Saints. However you should not fear as a born again believer because you have an in built lie detector. The Holy Spirit in you will testify and agree with truth and reject false hope built on shaky ground.

I write to you not because you are ignorant and do not perceive and know the Truth, but because you do perceive and know it, and [know positively] that nothing false (no deception, no lie) is of the Truth.
(1Jn 2:21 AMP)

Declaration

I declare that I will not be deceived by false hope. My Hope is based on Christ my rock in Jesus name. Amen

---

Hope is Hope, with God there is no such thing as false hope. There is no lie or deceit with the Lord, He sticks to His promises.

Hopeless Without The Word – Day 4

Do you see a man wise in his own eyes? There is more hope for a fool than for him.
(Pro 26:12 NIV)

Wisdom is of God. There is no one whether born again or not who can have wisdom without it coming from the Lord. The wisdom of God is in His Word which is true. There is no wisdom or power in a lie. Truth is of God and a lie is of the devil. Hope is an expectation based on a reason for that expectation. Hope in God is an expectation on the fulfillment of His Word. There is always Hope with God. Hopelessness is the absence of Hope. With God there is always Hope.

Whoever has their expectation on something other than the Word of God will be left hopeless. Our only Hope, trust and expectation must be on what God has said. Our opening scripture says a person who believes according to themselves that they are wise has less Hope than a fool. Now a fool is someone with limited wisdom. That means there isn't much of the Word of God a fool knows or acts on. The bible however shows us that the one who thinks they are wise according to their own judgment is worse off, than a fool. That is a person who does not consider the Word of God.
Whoever does not put their trust in the Word of God will receive hopelessness. That is they will be disappointed. Pin your Hope and expectation on the Word of God. What does the Word of God say?

It is better to trust in the LORD than to put confidence in man. (Psa 118:8 KJV)

The above scripture clearly shows us where we should put our trust. When we trust in the Lord we are holding on to His promises. Our focus and energy is all on what He has said and promised in His Word. This is the central chapter and verse in the bible. When the translators did this they did not know that this would be the exact middle of the bible. Coincidence? I think not this is divine. Hope in God.

The ungodly are not so, But are like the chaff which the wind drives away. Therefore the ungodly shall not stand in the judgment, Nor sinners in the congregation of the righteous. For the LORD knows the way of the righteous, But the way of the ungodly shall perish. (Psa 1:4-6 NKJV)

To have Hope in things contrary to the Word of God is similar to being an ungodly person. The ungodly have no Hope; they put their Hope in a lie filled with deceit. This why the bible says they shall perish because anything which is not in agreement with God's Word is hopeless.

Declaration

I declare that my Hope is firmly grounded on Jesus Christ and His Word. I only Hope in what is in agreement with the Word of God. I will not be left in a hopeless situation in my life because my trust is in the Lord. In Jesus name. Amen

Anything which is not in agreement with God's Word is hopeless.

Faith Needs Hope – Day 5

Now faith is the substance of things hoped for, the evidence of things not seen.

(Heb 11:1 KJV)

As you may already know faith is what we use to receive the promises of God. It is by faith that we access the power of God and make all things possible. However it is Hope that is loaded with 'the things'. In order for us to receive we must know what can be received. This is where Hope comes in. It is Hope that contains the potential for our life as Christians. Hope is the storehouse that faith needs.

The preaching of the Gospel is what reveals to us all that is contained in this wonderful treasure chest of the Lord. As you hear the good Word of the Lord everything that is possible is made known. The Word of Grace, the Word of Faith, the Word of Truth for an example all show what every believer should expect for their life. These messages show the expectation the Saints of God should have.

How then shall they call on him in whom they have not believed? and how shall they believe in him of whom they have not heard? and how shall they hear without a preacher? (Rom 10:14 KJV)

Those who hear the Gospel have their Hope made known to them. This is why it is important to have accurate knowledge of the promises of God. When you get to know what God has said is yours, you can believe correctly. An ignorant believer will believe wrongly. So build up your capacity to know the truth of God's promises.

My people are destroyed for lack of knowledge. Because you have rejected knowledge, I also will reject you from being priest for Me; Because you have forgotten the law of your God, I also will forget your children. (Hos 4:6 NKJV)

If one has no desire for truth and the Word of God their trust will be on something inadequate. Faith needs Hope. In order to access what is rightfully yours you should know the Hope you have in Christ. As you see and know the truth of God's promises to you, your faith can get a hold of what is meant for you.

So then faith comes by hearing, and hearing by the word of God. (Rom 10:17 NKJV)

For more on this read Forty Days On Faith by Jason Pullen

Confession

I confess that I will not be ignorant of the promises of God. I will get accurate knowledge on the promises of God so that my faith will be on truth in Jesus name. Amen

> **It is Hope that contains the potential for our life as Christians. Hope is the storehouse that faith needs.**

Saved By Hope – Day 6

For we are saved by hope: but hope that is seen is not hope: for what a man seeth, why doth he yet hope for? But if we hope for that we see not, *then* do we with patience wait for *it.*
(Rom 8:24-25 KJV)

Hope is the expectation for a promise of God to be fulfilled. One of the promises of God is salvation through faith in Jesus Christ. Salvation was made possible by Hope. There is a song which calls Jesus the Hope of the world. This is so true because this where the world and all of creation can find Hope (Salvation in Jesus Christ). But we must understand that once someone receives Jesus Christ they no longer Hope to be saved. They have been saved by their action of faith and God's supply of grace and mercy. All this however was made possible by the hope of being saved. Hope that wonderful link and container of the promises of God enables salvation.

Receiving the end of your faith, *even* the salvation of *your* souls. Of which salvation the prophets have enquired and searched diligently, who prophesied of the grace *that should come* unto you: Searching what, or what manner of time the Spirit of Christ which was

in them did signify, when it testified beforehand the sufferings of Christ, and the glory that should follow.
(1Pe 1:9-11 KJV)

The above scripture shows us that Hope kept this promise of Salvation, which was only possible after the death and resurrection of Jesus Christ. Now that Jesus has paid the price for Salvation anyone who acts in faith by confessing the Lordship of Jesus can be saved (the prayer of salvation). As our opening scripture stated what is not yet realized is hoped for but once it is seen and received it is no longer hoped for. For an unsaved person they have Hope of being saved. This is the amazing power of God, that there is always Hope for someone to be saved. Oh Praise the Lord!

Hope will always be there saying salvation is possible. By faith someone can access the greatest promise and be born again.

For by grace are ye saved through faith; and that not of yourselves: *it is* the gift of God: Not of works, lest any man should boast.
(Eph 2:8-9 KJV)

We thank Hope for being the storage and the link to what I believe to be the greatest promise of God; Salvation in Jesus Christ. We are saved by a combination of Hope, faith and grace.

Prayer

Thank you Father for granting me access to this great promise of Salvation. I pray for all those all over the world who have not yet received Salvation in Jesus Christ. That they will be saved by this Hope you have laid up for them in Jesus name. Amen

---
Hope that wonderful link and container of the promises of God enables salvation.

The Hope Of Salvation ~ Day 7

But let us, who are of the day, be sober, putting on
the breastplate of faith and love; and for an helmet,
the hope of salvation.

(1Th 5:8 KJV)

We received salvation by Hope, faith and grace. So what
exactly does the above scripture mean when it says we
should put on for a helmet the Hope of salvation? This is
not referring to one who is yet to be born again.
Remember this letter was written to born again believers,
the Thessalonians. The Holy Spirit here was making
reference to all the promises salvation brings. This is what
we should keep as a helmet. All the Word of God says we
are entitled to as Saints in the Kingdom of God; divine
health, prosperity, peace, power, redemption, freedom,
restitution, restoration and more.
These are some of the promises that come with salvation.
Every believer by faith has to draw these promises out
into existence in their life. Things will not just happen only
when a believer by faith grabs what is hoped for.

Therefore with joy shall ye draw water out of the
wells of salvation. And in that day shall ye say, Praise
the LORD, call upon his name, declare his doings
among the people, make mention that his name is
exalted. Sing unto the LORD; for he hath done
excellent things: this *is* known in all the earth.

(Isa 12:3-5 KJV)

When a thirsty person reaches a well of water/a water source they have Hope that their thirst will be quenched. This is the Hope of Salvation when access to a promise is granted. When this person gets a bucket and draws water from the well or opens the tap they enjoy the promise of God. One who is not born again does not have access to these wells. It is only the born again believers in Jesus Christ who have access to these wells of Salvation.

The Word of God explains salvation as a helmet in a soldier's armour. This is an important part of armour because it protects the head which is the control centre of a human. It is also the only part of the body that has the functioning of all five senses. By this you should realize the power of salvation. It is what enables us to hear, see, smell, taste and touch the things of God.

And take the helmet of salvation, and the sword of the Spirit, which is the word of God:
(Eph 6:17 KJV)

For more on this read Forty Days On Salvation by Jason Pullen

Declaration

I declare that I will enjoy the full benefits that salvation in Jesus Christ has made available to me.

The Word of God explains salvation as a helmet in a soldier's armour. This is an important part of armour because it protects the head which is the control centre of a human. It is also the only part of the body that has the functioning of all five senses. By this you should realize the power of salvation. It is what enables us to hear, see, smell, taste and touch the things of God.

Wait on the LORD: be of good courage, and he shall strengthen thine heart: wait, I say, on the LORD.
(Psa 27:14 KJV)

Waiting is something that is so powerful and necessary in life. There are some things of course which must be received immediately by faith such as healing. We see this throughout the gospels where Jesus would not permit someone to have a long wait while being tormented by demons; He would cast them out immediately. In other circumstances however waiting is necessary to match up with the perfect time of God. This is where Hope comes in.

Faith is our receiver of the things of God and Hope is the perfect waiter. It is because of Hope that we can wait for something to be fulfilled. We are enabled to wait because we know that our waiting is not in vain. Hope ensures us that something great will come at the appointed time.

I wait for the LORD, my soul doth wait, and in his word do I hope. My soul *waiteth* for the Lord more than they that watch for the morning: *I say, more than* they that watch for the morning. Let Israel hope in the LORD: for with the LORD *there is* mercy, and with him *is* plenteous redemption.
(Psa 130:5-7 KJV)

The disciples were told to wait in Jerusalem for the promise of the Father.

And being assembled together with them, **He commanded them not to depart from Jerusalem, but to wait for the Promise of the Father, "which," He** said, "you have heard from Me; "for John truly baptized with water, but you shall be baptized with the Holy Spirit not many days from now."
(Act 1:4-5 NKJV)

This is what they did and when the appointed time came, they received the baptism of the Holy Ghost.

When the Day of Pentecost had fully come, they were all with one accord in one place. And suddenly there came a sound from heaven, as of a rushing mighty wind, and it filled the whole house where they were sitting. Then there appeared to them divided tongues, as of fire, and one **sat upon each of them. And they were all filled with the Holy Spirit and began to speak with other tongues, as the Spirit gave them utterance.**
(Act 2:1-4 NKJV)

We must understand that some things will not come immediately but at an appointed season. This protects us from receiving something which is premature and weak. God knows when something must be birthed forth and Hope gives us strength during the waiting period.

The birth of Jesus Christ had to come at the perfect time. God could not just immediately send the Saviour, there was a perfect time. Until Jesus came the Israelites were kept by the Hope they had in the prophecies of a coming Saviour. They did not wait in pain or without expectation. They knew fully that redemption was coming.

But when the proper time had fully come, God sent His Son, born of a woman, born subject to [the regulations of] the Law, To purchase the freedom of (to ransom, to redeem, to atone for) those who were subject to the Law, that we might be adopted and have sonship conferred upon us [and be recognized as God's sons].
(Gal 4:4-5 AMP)

Waiting on God is not just the part of being patient for a fulfilled promise but about what you do during this time. The disciples on the day of Pentecost were in one accord, I believe they were praying. To wait on God also means to serve Him. This is similar to how a waiter attends to clients at a restaurant. A waiter is on standby to help the clients at their request. A butler; answers the door and attends to everyone who knocks at the door. An air hostess; is ready to serve passengers on a flight whenever they call. When we wait we serve the Lord according to His request.

Better is one day in your courts than a thousand elsewhere; I would rather be a doorkeeper in the house of my God than dwell in the tents of the wicked. (Psa 84:10 NIV)

We have the ability to wait on the Lord because of Hope our anchor and cord joining us to His Word of promise.

Prayer

Father my Hope and trust is in you and your Word. I will serve and worship you while I wait on you. For I know you keep your promises in Jesus name. Amen

---

Faith is our receiver of the things of God and Hope is the perfect waiter.

Patience Of Hope – Day 9

Remembering without ceasing your work of faith, and labour of love, and patience of hope in our Lord Jesus Christ, in the sight of God and our Father; Knowing, brethren beloved, your election of God.

(1Th 1:3-4 KJV)

Patience and Hope always go together, these two we can say are married. Patience is the ability to wait calmly without worry or anxiety. As a child of God we are able to wait on God without stress, worry or anxiety because we know our Hope in God will be fruitful.

And patience, experience; and experience, hope: And hope maketh not ashamed; because the love of God is shed abroad in our hearts by the Holy Ghost which is given unto us.

(Rom 5:4-5 KJV)

Whoever Hopes in the Lord will not be left disappointed. This is why we can confidently wait for God to answer a prayer or fulfill a prophetic Word He may have spoken to us. God is not a man to lie or shift from His promises. What He said to you, He will do. If the Lord says wait, then Hope and patience keep us calm and expectant.

And we desire that each one of you show the same diligence to the full assurance of hope until the end, that you do not become sluggish, but imitate those who through faith and patience inherit the promises.

(Heb 6:11-12 NKJV)

Patience enables one to remain diligent in waiting and serving the Lord. The majority of the children of Israel did not have patience to inherit the Promised Land because they had no Hope in God. We see this by how they complained and asked if they were brought to die in the desert.

Then they said to Moses, "Because there were **no graves in Egypt, have you taken us away to die in the wilderness? Why have you so dealt with us, to bring us up out of Egypt? "Is this not the word that we told you in Egypt, saying, 'Let us alone that we may serve the Egyptians?' For** it would have been **better for us to serve the Egyptians than that we should die in the wilderness."**
(Exo 14:11-12 NKJV)

Have a look at that. While they were still in Egypt they showed Moses they felt better to serve the Egyptians. They had more Hope in remaining as slaves than being freed by the Lord and serving Him. They did this despite how God had performed what were; wonders to them and plagues to the Egyptians. They did not have Hope; this is why they had no patience with Moses as the journey continued. Joshua and Caleb were the standouts who had Hope and therefore the ability to wait on God (serve Him).

Surely none of the men that came up out of Egypt, from twenty years old and upward, shall see the land which I sware unto Abraham, unto Isaac, and unto Jacob; because they have not wholly followed me: Save Caleb the son of Jephunneh the Kenezite, and

Joshua the son of Nun: for they have wholly followed the LORD. And the LORD'S anger was kindled against Israel, and he made them wander in the wilderness forty years, until all the generation, that had done evil in the sight of the LORD, was consumed.
(Num 32:11-13 KJV)

Moses the leader of the people and all those who were set free except Joshua and Caleb did not inherit the promise of God (The Promised Land). This was because they did not have patience. Moses was extremely patient but lost his patience along the way for just a moment and the Lord saw that as a slip up that cost him entering the Promised Land. Only Joshua and Caleb did not lose patience, react angrily or lose trust in God as they were firmly grounded in Hope of what God said.

Consider what the Lord has said to you through His Word and prophecies. Remain confident and at peace with this. Hold firm to Hope and you will not lose patience until you experience what God said. Patience has a role to play. We must allow it to work as we Hope in God.

My brethren, count it all joy when ye fall into divers temptations; Knowing *this,* that the trying of your faith worketh patience. But let patience have *her* perfect work, that ye may be perfect and entire, wanting nothing. (Jas 1:2-4 KJV)

For ye have need of patience, that, after ye have done the will of God, ye might receive the promise.
(Heb 10:36 KJV)

Declaration

I declare that my Hope is firmly grounded in Jesus Christ and everything He has said and will say to me. Therefore with the patience of Hope I will inherit everything He has laid up for me. In Jesus name. Amen

---

Patience enables one to remain diligent in waiting and serving the Lord.

No Worries With Hope - Day 10

"Therefore do not worry, saying, 'What shall we eat?' or 'What shall we drink?' or 'What shall we wear?' "For after all these things the Gentiles seek. For your heavenly Father knows that you need all these things. (Mat 6:31-32 NKJV)

The worry Jesus was dealing with in our theme scripture here was worry about the future. If Jesus taught on this it must mean that it was important. Jesus knew that people worry more about the future than the past or present. If you recall on day one of this book we understood that Hope is for the future. When we have Hope we have patience so that means we cannot worry or be anxious. We trust in what God said we will have in the future, even the immediate future like the next hour. Jesus promised He would provide for our future needs.

"Therefore I say to you, do not worry about your life, what you will eat or what you will drink; nor about your body, what you will put on. Is not life more than food and the body more than clothing? "Look at the birds of the air, for they neither sow nor reap nor gather into barns; yet your heavenly Father feeds them. Are you not of more value than they? (Mat 6:25-26 NKJV)

King Jesus said we are extremely valuable and should not worry about life's daily troubles. The unbelievers are concerned of such things but we are told to focus and seek the Kingdom of God and His righteousness. This means we should focus on doing what the Lord requires of us, which is to serve Him and not worry. Don't be concerned about the way the wicked live just look to Jesus for your prosperity and peace.

Rest in the LORD, and wait patiently for him: fret not thyself because of him who prospereth in his way, because of the man who bringeth wicked devices to pass. Cease from anger, and forsake wrath: fret not thyself in any wise to do evil. For evildoers shall be cut off: but those that wait upon the LORD, they shall inherit the earth.
(Psa 37:7-9 KJV)

As you serve King Jesus and His Kingdom you have a promise of the earth as your inheritance. If the earth is your inheritance how can you be worried about food, clothes, rent and the like. God knows every hair on your head, be at peace, you have good reason to expect provision, blessings and prosperity in your life.

Confession

I confess that I am loved by my heavenly Father. I will not worry for anything my future peace and prosperity is covered in Jesus name. Amen

---

As you serve King Jesus and His Kingdom you have a promise of the earth as your inheritance. If the earth is your inheritance how can you be worried about food, clothes, rent and the like.

I have set the LORD always before me: because *he is* at my right hand, I shall not be moved. Therefore my heart is glad, and my glory rejoiceth: my flesh also shall rest in hope.

(Psa 16:8-9 KJV)

Hope is also a resting place. Rest is a good way to recover from being tired but someone can rest even when they are not tired. God created the heavens and the earth in six days and then rested on the seventh not because He was tired just because He saw it was good to rest.

Our opening verse is a prophetic word concerning Jesus Christ; that His flesh would rest in Hope and not see corruption. When Jesus died He was put in a tomb but went to hell and rose again with the same physical body. He had the Hope that His body would not decay and it did not.

Therefore being a prophet, and knowing that God had sworn with an oath to him, that of the fruit of his loins, according to the flesh, he would raise up Christ to sit on his throne; He seeing this before spake of the resurrection of Christ, that his soul was not left in hell, neither his flesh did see corruption. (Act 2:30-31 KJV)

There is a similar Hope for believers who have died in Christ that their corrupt bodies will put on incorruption. That means every person who died physically has a Hope of resurrection with a renewed body.

For this corruptible must put on incorruption, and this mortal *must* put on immortality.
(1Co 15:53 KJV)

For those who have fallen asleep (died) they rest in Hope of the resurrection. We who are alive also rest in Hope for what we desire to see in our lives. We are not anxious, troubled or weary in all our trials and tribulations. We can be calm and at peace in the storm because Hope keeps us at peace. When you know the end result will be good you can rest and wait patiently. If we were unsure of the future then we would have no peace and rest.

Why art thou cast down, O my soul? and why art thou disquieted within me? hope in God: for I shall yet praise him, *who is* the health of my countenance, and my God. (Psa 43:5 KJV)

Whenever there is rest there is peace and Joy. As Christians as we trust and believe the Word of God we are at peace and Joy. Paul wrote letters to Christians while in prison. Yet in those letters he expresses peace and unspeakable Joy that he has. An ordinary human being would be troubled and anxious in prison but not Apostle Paul. Be at peace God is with you always.

Declaration

I declare that I will rest in Hope. The Lord Jesus is with me always therefore I will rest and be at peace in Life in Jesus name. Amen

Rejoice In Hope – Day 12

Be kindly affectioned one to another with brotherly love; in honour preferring one another; Not slothful in business; fervent in spirit; serving the Lord; Rejoicing in hope; patient in tribulation; continuing instant in prayer; Distributing to the necessity of saints; given to hospitality. (Rom 12:10-13 KJV)

The Word of God is filled with instructions which guide us in life. The love of God is the greatest power we have. It is the force that gives us life and fuels all of creation. One of the things we are instructed to do, is to rejoice in Hope. What does it mean to rejoice in Hope? Celebrate the promises of God. Sing, dance and celebrate that your heavenly Father has a good plan for you. Do not be saddened by a past event or present situation. Be filled with joy that the Lord is going to work something good for your future.

For I know the plans I have for you," declares the LORD, "plans to prosper you and not to harm you, plans to give you hope and a future.
(Jer 29:11 NIV)

If someone were to show you the plans they have for you for a new house they intend to give you, would you not rejoice? If your employer was to show you a good future position they have for you with great benefits after you reach some easy goals, would you not rejoice? I believe you would. This is what the bible means when it says rejoice in Hope. When you think of God's plans and thought towards you, you ought to celebrate. It is only someone who has no promise that could be sad. Not so with a child of God. Rejoice in Hope!

By whom also we have access by faith into this grace wherein we stand, and rejoice in hope of the glory of God. (Rom 5:2 KJV)

There is the Hope of the Glory of God. What is the Glory of God? It is the weight of His splendor, nature and excellence. When the Glory of God is present things are so easy, peaceful, joyful and wonderful. This is what we as believers must be joyfully expectant of in our lives and in every situation.

My brethren, count it all joy when ye fall into divers temptations; Knowing *this*, that the trying of your faith worketh patience. (Jas 1:2-3 KJV)

This seems crazy from a normal person to understand. How can someone rejoice when they are faced with a problematic situation? We all face various trials in life and some which seem irrecoverable. For an example someone may say I've lost a loved one; how can I rejoice in Hope. Other terrible situations may happen to someone being fired, a reputation ruined and the like. I want to tell you there is and there always will be Hope!

Regardless of how dark your life may seem to be. The answer is to rejoice in Hope! You may say I don't even have strength to rejoice in Hope. Praise the Lord for He said when you are weak He is strong. He will strengthen you and when He does, rejoice in Hope! The beginning is just to hear the Word of God. What is God saying? He says He will strengthen you and turn you mourning into dancing, your night into day. That's sufficient. From there you will experience the Power of God. Keep Jesus as your Hope; trust in Him, His Hope is a solid supernatural, eternal rock that cannot be moved.

He has sent me to proclaim That the time has come When the LORD will save his people And defeat their enemies. He has sent me to comfort all who mourn, To give to those who mourn in Zion Joy and gladness instead of grief, A song of praise instead of sorrow. They will be like trees That the LORD himself has planted. They will all do what is right, And God will be praised for what he has done. (Isa 61:2-3 GNB)

Be filled with joy because your trust in King Jesus Christ is not in vain. Where you thought you could never recover or have joy, you will. There is an expectation for all children of God to enjoy the goodness and Glory of God here in this life.

Then he answered and spake unto me, saying, This *is* the word of the LORD unto Zerubbabel, saying, Not by might, nor by power, but by my spirit, saith the LORD of hosts. (Zec 4:6 KJV)

Act

Always be joyful expecting the Glory of God in your life!

Celebrate the promises of God. Sing, dance and celebrate that your heavenly Father has a good plan for you.

Hope In The Day Of evil- Day 13

Be not a terror unto me: thou *art* my hope in the day of evil. (Jer 17:17 KJV)

Our opening verse has a wonderful lamentation from the Prophet Jeremiah. He knew all about the wrath of God and saw the result of those who forsook the Lord. This is why He said Lord don't be a terror to me. He knew that when trouble comes His Hope was the Lord. As a child of God one thing you should know is that the Lord never brings you pain and suffering. He has no desire to hurt His children or teach them with a painful experience. When a wicked attack comes, it is the Lord who we should trust to get us out of it.

If we are tempted by such trials, we must not say, "This temptation comes from God." For God cannot be tempted by evil, and he himself tempts no one. (Jas 1:13 GNB)

How God anointed Jesus of Nazareth with the Holy Ghost and with power: who went about doing good, and healing all that were oppressed of the devil; for God was with him. (Act 10:38 KJV)

From these scriptures above we can see that it is the devil that afflicts with pain and sickness. Even death is not from God. The bible describes it as an enemy. These are all things that try and stop children of God; attacks that come in the wicked day of evil. But the Lord is able to help us.

For he must reign, till he hath put all enemies under his feet. The last enemy *that* **shall be destroyed** *is* **death.**
(1Co 15:25-26 KJV)

"The thief does not come except to steal, and to kill, and to destroy. I have come that they may have life, and that they may have it more abundantly.
(Joh 10:10 NKJV)

Jesus faced the evil day when His time for crucifixion had arrived. However He found strength and comfort from the angel of the Lord. Even though this was a terrible dark day and Jesus had to go through it, He still had Hope and strength from the Father.

"When I was with you daily in the temple, you did not try to seize Me. But this is your hour, and the power of darkness."
(Luk 22:53 NKJV)

Saying, "Father, if it is Your will, take this cup away from Me; nevertheless not My will, but Yours, be done." **Then an angel appeared to Him from heaven, strengthening Him.**
(Luk 22:42-43 NKJV)

Jesus had to go through with the crucifixion, which He identified as the hour and power of darkness. As believers in Jesus Christ the evil day may come but we do not have to be crucified because Jesus was crucified for us. Just as how Abraham did not have to offer his son Isaac because the Lord had provided the sacrifice. When we maintain Hope in the Lord we overcome all trials thrown at us by the enemy because the Father provided a way out, He provided the sacrifice. Hallelujah!

And Isaac spake unto Abraham his father, and said, My father: and he said, Here *am* I, my son. And he said, Behold the fire and the wood: but where *is* the lamb for a burnt offering? And Abraham said, My son, God will provide himself a lamb for a burnt offering: so they went both of them together.

(Gen 22:7-8 KJV)

Our heavenly Father will never leave us nor forsake us. He is with us always. In the darkness He is there. He tells us to stand still and not fight. As the Holy Spirit spoke to King Jehoshaphat and the children of Israel when they seemed doomed. Stand still and see the Salvation of the Lord. The Holy Spirit also spoke through Moses at the Red sea when death seemed to be eminent to Stand still and see the Salvation of the Lord. If an attack comes, trust in the Lord, Stand Still; Jesus is your Hope in the evil day.

Wherefore take unto you the whole armour of God, that ye may be able to withstand in the evil day, and having done all, to stand.

(Eph 6:13 KJV)

Stand, do not fight but stand trusting in Jesus holding His Word, speaking His Word. The Lord will deliver out of every trap the enemy sets, this is our firm Hope.

There hath no temptation taken you but such as is common to man: but God *is* faithful, who will not suffer you to be tempted above that ye are able; but will with the temptation also make a way to escape, that ye may be able to bear *it.*
(1Co 10:13 KJV)

Prayer

Father you are my Hope in all times especially in times of trouble. I trust that you will always strengthen me and make a way out for me in the evil day in Jesus name. Amen

---

Our heavenly Father will never leave us nor forsake us. He is with us always. In the darkness He is there. He tells us to stand still and not fight.

Hope Endures The Test ~ Day 14

By faith Abraham, when he was tested, offered up Isaac, and he who had received the promises offered up his only begotten son, of whom it was said, "In Isaac your seed shall be called," concluding that God was able to raise him up, even from the dead, from which he also received him in a figurative sense. (Heb 11:17-19 NKJV)

Abraham is our father of faith because he is the one revealed to us who truly lived by faith. There were others before him who did live by faith in God but the Lord chose him. Abraham's faith was greatly tested when God told him to offer Isaac, his child of promise as a sacrifice. The scriptures show us that Abraham knew that God could raise Isaac back to life even if he had sacrificed him. This was faith. Abraham represents faith but Isaac represents Hope and the promise of God. Isaac had a different experience to Abraham during this test.

Abraham placed the wood for the burnt offering on Isaac's shoulders, while he himself carried the knife and the fire. As the two of them went on together, Isaac said, "Father?" "Yes, my son," Abraham replied. "We have the wood and the fire," said the boy, "but where is the lamb for the sacrifice?" "God will provide a lamb, my son," Abraham answered. And they both went on together. (Gen 22:6-8 NLT)

At this moment Isaac saw there was no sacrifice. Little did he know that he was the planned sacrifice! Isaac just had to trust in the words of his father Abraham, that the Lord will provide the sacrifice. Remember Isaac represents Hope. The Hope for a nation was in Isaac. A nation that would be God's people and bless the world. This Hope was put fully to test.

When they came to the place which God had told him about, Abraham built an altar and arranged the wood on it. He tied up his son and placed him on the altar, on top of the wood. Then he picked up the knife to kill him. But the angel of the LORD called to him from heaven, "Abraham, Abraham!" He answered, "Yes, here I am." "Don't hurt the boy or do anything to him," he said. "Now I know that you honor and obey God, because you have not kept back your only son from him."
(Gen 22:9-12 GNB)

Hope endured this trial. Isaac endured this trial. Isaac was a young boy not a baby or a toddler, he fully understood what was happening. I'm certain Isaac cried, kicked, screamed and fought his father Abraham when he was bound to the altar. If Isaac was willing to go along with the plan there would have been no reason for Abraham to tie him up. Isaac probably thought Abraham had lost his mind. However the Lord fulfilled His promise and provided the lamb for the sacrifice.

And he said, Lay not thine hand upon the lad, neither do thou any thing unto him: for now I know that thou fearest God, seeing thou hast not withheld thy son, thine only *son* from me. And Abraham lifted up his eyes, and looked, and behold behind *him* a ram caught in a thicket by his horns: and Abraham went

and took the ram, and offered him up for a burnt offering in the stead of his son. And Abraham called the name of that place Jehovahjireh: as it is said *to* this day, In the mount of the LORD it shall be seen.
(Gen 22:12-14 KJV)

Of all the tests Isaac went through in his life, I believe nearly being sacrificed by his father Abraham was the toughest. From this we understand that Hope in God is able to overcome the most difficult trials in life. We may face trials where even the closest people we depend on are against us and about to kill us. God can still turn that scenario around. Hope carries us through the storm.

When you pass through the waters, I will be with you; and through the rivers, they shall not overflow you. When you walk through the fire, you shall not be burned; nor shall the flame kindle on you.
(Isa 43:2 MKJV)

Isaac who represents Hope and the promise of God went through the test. He did not hate Abraham after this but had a deeper revelation of God. You too can go through the test because you have the Hope of the Lord.

Confession

I confess that the Hope of the Lord will keep me and carry me through any trial in life. My Hope in Jesus Christ endures all things and prevails in Jesus name. Amen

> **Of all the tests Isaac went through in his life, I believe nearly being sacrificed by his father Abraham was the toughest. From this we understand that Hope in God is able to overcome the most difficult trials in life.**

Strength Renewed By Hope – Day 15

Even the youths shall faint and be weary, and the young men shall utterly fall: But they that wait upon the LORD shall renew *their* strength; they shall mount up with wings as eagles; they shall run, and not be weary; *and* they shall walk, and not faint.
(Isa 40:30-31 KJV)

We all need strength daily, whether it is mental, emotional or physical strength. We need strength each and every day of our lives. All strength stems from spiritual strength. Remember God is Spirit and the source of all life. Spiritual strength feeds all other forms of strength.

God *is* a Spirit: and they that worship him must worship *him* in spirit and in truth.
(Joh 4:24 KJV)

Isaiah states that even young people can become weary but those who wait on the Lord will renew their strength. Our opening verse says those who wait on the Lord will mount up with wings as eagles. Why an eagle? On day eight of this book we understood that Hope enables us to wait on the Lord; meaning to serve or attend to Him like a waiter. An eagle is one unique bird, an animal that the

Word of God often makes reference to. We'll understand why.

An eagle does not waste energy flapping its wings continually as other birds. An eagle is at rest when in flight it simply soars, using opposing winds to fly. By this it is able to preserve its energy and fly higher than most birds. It even has the ability to use violent winds to soar higher than thunderstorms. Now the bible says when you wait on the Lord you will soar like an eagle effortlessly. Every storm will be a stepping stone and fuel to empower you to rise above it. This is what an eagle does.

On day eleven we saw what resting in Hope is all about. An eagle is at rest when it flies. The stronger the wind the better it is for an eagle. Hope renews your strength.

He gives strength to the weary and increases the power of the weak. Even youths grow tired and weary, and young men stumble and fall; but those who hope in the LORD will renew their strength. They will soar on wings like eagles; they will run and not grow weary, they will walk and not be faint.
(Isa 40:29-31 NIV)

It is normal for an elderly person to get tired faster than a younger person. However the bible promises that Hoping in the Lord renews strength such that an older person can have more energy and vigour than a younger person. This is where the science of an eagle comes in again.

Who satisfies your mouth with good things, So that your youth is renewed like the eagle's.
(Psa 103:5 NKJV)

The Word of God promises youth renewal. What does this mean? It means age reversal. This is the renewal of strength where someone's natural body becomes younger. You may say where did this happen. We see Sarah who after her husband had no desire to be with her was picked as a beautiful lady for the King. Kings do not pick old women but young good looking women. This can only mean that Sarah's youth was renewed and this is how she gave birth to the child of promise Isaac. Sarah was not a pregnant hunched, wrinkled old woman as some think.

Abraham and Sarah were old. Sarah was past the age of childbearing. And so Sarah laughed to herself, thinking, "Now that I've become old, will I enjoy myself again? What's more, my husband is old!"
(Gen 18:11-12 GW)

And Abraham said of Sarah his wife, She is my sister. And Abimelech king of Gerar sent and took Sarah [into his harem].
(Gen 20:2 AMP)

In Genesis chapter eighteen Sarah laughed at the thought of having children with Abraham as they were both old. Later in Genesis chapter twenty the King chose Sarah for his harem. This clearly shows her youth was renewed and she had a sexy appearance to the king.

An eagle at around age forty has a choice where it can renew its youth and strength or die. An eagle fly's high and plucks out its old feathers breaks its talons and smashes its beak off. After about one hundred and fifty days the eagle grows new lighter feathers, talons and a new beak. This enables the eagle to live about another thirty years. This is the wisdom of the Lord when he says He will renew your strength like an eagle. This is possible by Hoping in the promises of God.

Abraham after Sarah passed still had other children testifying that he too had youth renewal. Joshua held on to the promises of God. His Hope in the Lord kept him strong and renewed. When you still believe to see the fulfillment of God's promises you have strength, a reason to live and you will be strong. It is a lie that you ought to age and become weak. Your time has passed they may say. That is a lie, be like Joshua who at eighty five was as strong as a young man.

"So look at me. The LORD has kept me alive as he promised. It's been 45 years since Israel wandered in the desert when the LORD made this promise to Moses. So now look at me today. I'm 85 years old. I'm still as fit to go to war now as I was when Moses sent me out. Now give me this mountain region which the LORD spoke of that day. You heard that the people of Anak are still there and that they have large, fortified cities. If the LORD is with me, I can force them out, as he promised."

(Jos 14:10-12 GW)

Moses also had his strength constantly renewed he did not die of old age. The Lord had to command him at one hundred and twenty years to die.

"Go up this mountain of the Abarim, Mount Nebo, which is in the land of Moab, across from Jericho; view the land of Canaan, which I give to the children of Israel as a possession; "and die on the mountain which you ascend, and be gathered to your people, just as Aaron your brother died on Mount Hor and was gathered to his people; "because you trespassed against Me among the children of Israel at the waters of Meribah Kadesh, in the Wilderness of Zin, because you did not hallow Me in the midst of the children of Israel.
(Deu 32:49-51 NKJV)

Moses was 120 years old when he died, yet his eyesight was clear, and he was as strong as ever.
(Deu 34:7 NLT)

An eagle has remarkable eyesight. This is what you should expect like Moses, his Hope in God kept him strong despite the hard hearted and stiff necked people he had to lead daily. If you are a leader never say people are taking your strength, they can't no matter how bad they are. An eagle has staying power. Its endurance, renewal of youth and strength is ours as believers in Jesus. An eagle also keeps one mate for life. That is a marriage. There is renewal in marriage. God is good. As you Hope in Him there is renewal like an eagle.

Declaration

I declare that my Hope in the Lord Jesus Christ and His promises renews my strength and my youth. I will not grow old or weary. I am strengthened daily by the Holy Spirit in Jesus name. Amen

---

Now the bible says when you wait on the Lord you will soar like an eagle effortlessly. Every storm will be a stepping stone and fuel to empower you to rise above it.

Re: Facts on Eagles

https://www.10000birds.com/the-eagles-rebirth-yep-seriously.htm

https://chirpforbirds.com/avian-inspiration/10-amazing-facts-about-bald-eagles/

https://a-z-animals.com/blog/discover-just-how-high-eagles-can-soar/

And the LORD turned the captivity of Job, when he prayed for his friends: also the LORD gave Job twice as much as he had before.
(Job 42:10 KJV)

The story of Job is filled with much wisdom of God. We must always remember that everything that was written in the Word of God was for us to learn from. It does not mean that everything that took place was correct or what God desired.

Everything written in the Scriptures was written to teach us, in order that we might have hope through the patience and encouragement which the Scriptures give us.
(Rom 15:4 GNB)

We learn from the book of Job of a man who was the wealthiest in the land and feared God. Trouble came when he feared the loss of all and would continually offer sacrifices thinking God would judge his children for their wickedness. The man then lost everything in record time and was reduced to a vagabond filled with sickness but alive.

The morning after each feast, Job would get up early and offer sacrifices for each of his children in order to purify them. He always did this because he thought that one of them might have sinned by insulting God unintentionally. (Job 1:5 GNB)

For the thing which I greatly feared is come upon me, and that which I was afraid of is come unto me. I was not in safety, neither had I rest, neither was I quiet; yet trouble came.
(Job 3:25-26 KJV)

Job suffered great loss because of his fear. God did not take from him or give satan power to destroy him as a test. The Lord just said to satan, Job's fear had given him the right to destroy. Job feared losing all and that's what he got. In his ignorance he thought the Lord had taken from him.

Then his wife said to him, "Do you still hold fast to your integrity? Curse God and die!" But he said to her, "You speak as one of the foolish women speaks. Shall we indeed accept good from God, and shall we not accept adversity?" In all this Job did not sin with his lips.
(Job 2:9-10 NKJV)

In spite of Job thinking the Lord brought evil upon him. He would not curse God. He still worshipped the Lord. His friends thought he must have sinned for such evil to come upon him. At the end of it all the Lord rebuked Job for thinking the destruction came from Him. He defended Job in front of His friends and rebuked them more for accusing Job. At the end of it all when Job prayed for his three friends that accused him, He was restored.

And the LORD restored Job's losses when he prayed for his friends. Indeed the LORD gave Job twice as much as he had before. (Job 42:10 NKJV)

Even though Job did not understand what had caused his loss, he held unto God. He worshipped the Lord not knowing that He had Hope. He simply said if this is what God has given me, I just have to take it. The Lord had not given it to him. The Lord had protected him but when the enemy realized Job's fear had given him an opportunity, he pounced. The faithfulness of God however restored Job to double for what he had lost.

This is what Hope in the Lord makes certain, restoration for all that is lost. Maybe in life you've lost money, peace, health, a loved one and the like. Be confident that your Hope in Jesus will bring restoration of all that was lost. Although Job was ignorant, he was patient. In the end He saw the hand of God.

Now the LORD blessed the latter days of Job more than his beginning; for he had fourteen thousand sheep, six thousand camels, one thousand yoke of oxen, and one thousand female donkeys.
(Job 42:12 NKJV)

Behold, we count them happy which endure. Ye have heard of the patience of Job, and have seen the end of the Lord; that the Lord is very pitiful, and of tender mercy.
(Jas 5:11 KJV)

Hope in the Lord, is also trust that whatever was stolen will be paid back. Hope does not accept loss as final but says there is better coming at the end of the story.

And I will restore to you the years that the locust hath eaten, the cankerworm, and the caterpiller, and the palmerworm, my great army which I sent among you. And ye shall eat in plenty, and be satisfied, and praise the name of the LORD your God, that hath dealt wondrously with you: and my people shall never be ashamed. And ye shall know that I *am* in the midst of Israel, and *that* I *am* the LORD your God, and none else: and my people shall never be ashamed.
(Joe 2:25-27 KJV)

Confession

I confess that I have a guarantee of restoration for loss in my life or anything that pertains to me. My Hope in Jesus speaks of me receiving double for my trouble in Jesus name. Amen

---

Hope does not accept loss as final but says there is better coming at the end of the story.

Hope Multiplies Hope ~ Day 17

For the promise is unto you, and to your children, and to all that are afar off, *even* as many as the Lord our God shall call.

(Act 2:39 KJV)

Sowing and reaping is a wonderful Kingdom truth and principle. We get what we give, we harvest what we plant. Whoever trusts in the Lord will harvest the good fruit of that. The Hope that one person has in the Lord will cause many people to Hope in God too. The Lord began a promise with Abraham.

And I will make you exceedingly fruitful, greatly so, and I will make nations of you, and kings shall come out of you. And I will establish My covenant between Me and you and your seed after you in their generations for an everlasting covenant, to be a God to you and to your seed after you.

(Gen 17:6-7 MKJV)

The Lord gave Hope to Abraham and to his seed (his descendants). By Abraham accepting the Word of God and Hoping in Him, his child Isaac and grandchild Jacob held on in strong Hope. This is a great example of Hope multiplied.

Reside in this land, and I will be with you and bless you. For to you and to your seed I will give all these lands; and I will establish the oath which I swore to Abraham your father. And I will make your seed to

multiply as the stars of the heavens, and will give to your seed all these lands. And in your Seed shall all the nations of the earth be blessed, because Abraham obeyed My voice and kept My charge, My commandments, My statutes, and My Laws.
(Gen 26:3-5 MKJV)

Isaac enjoyed the benefits of the Hope his father Abraham had in God. Isaac saw that it was beneficial to wait and trust in the Lord from seeing God's faithfulness to his father. As a result Isaac also held on to the promises of God. Jacob his son did the same and enjoyed the fruit of serving the Lord.

And God said to him, Your name is Jacob. Your name shall not be called Jacob any more, but Israel shall be your name. And He called his name Israel. And God said to him, I am God Almighty. Be fruitful and multiply. A nation and a company of nations shall be from you, and kings shall come out of your loins.
(Gen 35:10-11 MKJV)

From Jacob came the children of Israel who became a nation. After that through Christ all believers are partakers of this Hope multiplied. As an individual giving your life to Hope in God and his promises can cause your friends and family members to Hope in God too. This will transform families, communities, nations and the world.

Prayer

Dear Father may my Hope in you be multiplied to affect my family, friends, community and the world over for generations to come in Jesus name. Amen

The Promise; Isaac Not Ishmael – Day 18

And Abraham said unto God, O that Ishmael might live before thee! And God said, Sarah thy wife shall bear thee a son indeed; and thou shalt call his name Isaac: and I will establish my covenant with him for an everlasting covenant, *and* with his seed after him. (Gen 17:18-19 KJV)

The Lord had told Abram that he would have an heir from himself. The first time God reminded Abram of this he did not have any children, Ishmael was not yet born. Abram believed but only had a slave as an heir.

Afterward the LORD spoke to Abram in a vision and said to him, "Do not be afraid, Abram, for I will protect you, and your reward will be great." But Abram replied, "O Sovereign LORD, what good are all your blessings when I don't even have a son? Since I don't have a son, Eliezer of Damascus, a servant in my household, will inherit all my wealth. You have given me no children, so one of my servants will have to be my heir." Then the LORD said to him, "No, your servant will not be your heir, for you will have a son of your own to inherit everything I am giving you." (Gen 15:1-4 NLT)

What mattered to Abram was the continuance of his name. This is what any normal man would want; for his children to continue with the family name and be greater than them. It is painful when a man is so successful without a son to give the inheritance to. This is what got to Abram. He was extremely prosperous, wealthy and successful but had no child to give it all to. He lamented that one of his servants would benefit. The Lord assured Abram to Hope in His promise, a son was coming.

Sarai Abram's wife aware of the frustrations of her husband and the promise God gave him had a plan. She interpreted that Abram receiving an heir maybe didn't involve her as his wife. Ignorantly she tried to help God keep His word and gave Hagar as a wife to Abram.

So Sarai said to Abram, "See now, the LORD has restrained me from bearing children. Please, go in to my maid; perhaps I shall obtain children by her." And Abram heeded the voice of Sarai.
(Gen 16:2 NKJV)

When the Lord gives a promise we must hold on in Hope and not try and assist the Lord or make a plan B. This was not the plan of God but the plan of man. As our opening verse explained, that God's promise was to Abram and his wife Sarai. Abram thought he had to settle for Ishmael a child of a slave.
Do not settle for something which can be achieved by mans strength. The promise of God requires Hope in God not man. The original plan of God was Isaac not Ishmael. It was easy for Ishmael to come along but looked

impossible for Isaac to come. Yet Abram held on to Hope that somehow Isaac is going to come.

As a child of God this is what you should do. Hold on in Hope for the original promise of God; Isaac. Let God bring it to pass. At times people err by working something in their own strength and produce an Ishmael. That imitation of the promise of God can become a problem as Ishmael became.

Wait for the genuine thing, don't settle for less. It may be a marriage partner you are waiting for, don't settle for Ishmael, wait for Isaac. It may be an investor for your business, wait for Isaac don't settle for Ishmael. If ever you made a mistake and manufactured an Ishmael cast it away so Isaac can have his true place.

When Isaac comes you will know its Isaac. When you receive the genuine original plan of God (Isaac) you will know it is the promise.

Nevertheless what saith the scripture? Cast out the bondwoman and her son: for the son of the bondwoman shall not be heir with the son of the freewoman.
(Gal 4:30 KJV)

When Sarah saw that Ishmael mocked Isaac she demanded him to be cast out. He was then cast away as he was not the rightful heir. He was an illegitimate child. If there ever happens to be something illegitimate competing with the genuine blessing of God in your life, get rid of it. It may a business that is functioning by corruption, yet the Lord has brought the real business He promised you, close the fake one.

Ishmael was Abraham's first born but born of a slave woman whom he had no desire for. He had other children but his only child he saw as his true child was Isaac from Sarah the woman he loved his wife. This is why Abraham left all he had to Isaac and made sure the other children were separated from Isaac.

And Abraham gave all that he had to Isaac. But to the sons of his concubines [Hagar and Keturah] Abraham gave gifts, and while he was still living he sent them to the east country, away from Isaac his son [of promise]. (Gen 25:5-6 AMP)

With whatever you are dealing with in your life. Check, is this the promise of God or am I dealing with a quick fix or plan B. When its Isaac you will have no doubt this is Isaac. Give your all to the promise of God.

Act

Wait for Isaac and give everything to him.

The promise of God requires Hope in God not man. The original plan of God was Isaac not Ishmael. It was easy for Ishmael to come along but looked impossible for Isaac to come.

Children of Promise – Day 19

And you, dear brothers and sisters, are children of the
promise, just like Isaac.
(Gal 4:28 NLT)

Abraham was given a promise from the Lord that from
Isaac would come a mighty people. Isaac was the child of
promise. When a dispute rose between Sarah and Hagar,
the Lord told Abraham to listen to Sarah. Ishmael was cast
out as Sarah requested. Ishmael was a child of the flesh
one born out of man's carnal idea. This was not the plan
or promise of God but a poor attempt to help God fulfill
His oath. This is why the Lord said Ishmael is not my plan
but I will bless him also, Isaac is my plan. We are God's
plan.

**And she said to Abraham, "Get rid of that slave
woman and her son, for that slave woman's son will
never share in the inheritance with my son Isaac." The
matter distressed Abraham greatly because it
concerned his son. But God said to him, "Do not be so
distressed about the boy and your maidservant. Listen
to whatever Sarah tells you, because it is through Isaac
that your offspring will be reckoned.**
(Gen 21:10-12 NIV)

Isaac was a result of the Word of promise God had
spoken. Ishmael was a result of the idea of Sarah to fulfill
God's promise. The Lord rejected that as not being His
plan. Ironically Sarah who hatched the plan was the one
who firmly wanted the fruit of her idea gone! What does
this all mean to us?

A child of God is not a child of God because of the flesh. This means it is not the direct descendants of Abraham through Isaac who are the heirs to the promise of Abraham. The Israelites (Jews) according to the flesh are the seed of Abraham but believers in Jesus Christ are the rightful heirs the Lord spoke about.

But it is not that the word of God has taken no effect. For they are not all Israel who are of Israel, nor are they all children because they are the seed of Abraham; but, "In Isaac your seed shall be called." That is, those who are the children of the flesh, these are not the children of God; but the children of the promise are counted as the seed.
(Rom 9:6-8 NKJV)

Now to Abraham and his seed were the promises made. He saith not, And to seeds, as of many; but as of one, And to thy seed, which is Christ.
(Gal 3:16 KJV)

Our Hope is in Christ. It is Jesus Christ who the Father was speaking of when He said to Abraham, I will make your seed a blessing to all. We have received the fulfillment of this promise. Once Christ came and became a sacrifice on the cross salvation was possible. Now that we are born again and saved we are connected to the bloodline of Christ. Christians are part of the Christ family and heirs to the promise made to Abraham. We are the children of promise.

That in blessing I will bless thee, and in multiplying I will multiply thy seed as the stars of the heaven, and

as the sand which *is* upon the sea shore; and thy seed
shall possess the gate of his enemies; And in thy seed
shall all the nations of the earth be blessed; because
thou hast obeyed my voice.
(Gen 22:17-18 KJV)

This promise is to believers in Jesus Christ not the Jewish
people alone. The promise was given to them in the flesh
and the Israelites have been blessed because of it.
However the promise of the Spirit is greater. There is no
reason to check whether you have a Jewish ancestor or
not. To be born again in Jesus Christ is greater; this is how
to become a child of God. Being an Israelite does not
make someone a child of God.

There is neither Jew nor Greek, there is neither bond
nor free, there is neither male nor female: for ye are
all one in Christ Jesus. And if ye *be* Christ's, then are ye
Abraham's seed, and heirs according to the promise.
(Gal 3:28-29 KJV)

We have access to this promise and must stand to see
believers in Jesus Christ bless all nations. We are to
possess the gates of our enemies, lend to nations and
multiply. This is our Hope in Christ to rule the world with
compassion. A child of God was not created to be the
subject of oppression but to remove the oppressor and
lead with love and compassion like Jesus did.

The LORD shall open unto thee his good treasure, the
heaven to give the rain unto thy land in his season,
and to bless all the work of thine hand: and thou shalt

lend unto many nations, and thou shalt not borrow.
(Deu 28:12 KJV)

And they sung a new song, saying, Thou art worthy to
take the book, and to open the seals thereof: for thou
wast slain, and hast redeemed us to God by thy blood
out of every kindred, and tongue, and people, and
nation; And hast made us unto our God kings and
priests: and we shall reign on the earth.
(Rev 5:9-10 KJV)

Declaration

I declare that I am an heir to the promise God made to
Abraham. I am a child of God a King and Priest in me
shall all nations be blessed in Jesus name. Amen

**Christians are part of the Christ family and
heirs to the promise made to Abraham. We
are the children of promise.**

And I will bless her, and give thee a son also of her:
yea, I will bless her, and she shall be *a mother* of
nations; kings of people shall be of her. Then Abraham
fell upon his face, and laughed, and said in his heart,
Shall *a child* be born unto him that is an hundred years
old? and shall Sarah, that is ninety years old, bear?
(Gen 17:16-17 KJV)

Have you ever laughed so much that you fall down? This
is what happened to Abraham when the Lord reminded
Him of His promise of a child with Sarah. The bible tells us
Abraham believed God but somehow he still laughed at
the thought of the promise being fulfilled here. He was
rolling with laughter. Has the Lord ever promised you
something which you laughed at ever happening?

At times I've given prophecies and the receiver or hearers
laugh, saying how will this happen? Thank God His Word
of promise doesn't depend on man.

The Hope of God brings joy! People may laugh
spontaneously not knowing why. The joy is a
confirmation of the Spirit man. The mind may not receive
it but the Spirit man does. Abraham did not doubt but
found himself laughing. He was not mocking God but
laughed to say, how will it happen?

We see the prophet Elisha declaring something which
seemed so far-fetched and crazy. Any normal person
probably laughed at this proclamation of poverty ending
over night. An officer found it so hilarious and made a

joke of this promise. This officer did not believe the Word of promise and mocked the prophet for what he saw as 'false Hope'. (See day 3)

Then Elisha said, "Hear the word of the LORD. Thus says the LORD: 'Tomorrow about this time a seah of fine flour shall be sold for a shekel, and two seahs of barley for a shekel, at the gate of Samaria.'" So an officer on whose hand the king leaned answered the man of God and said, "Look, if the LORD would make windows in heaven, could this thing be?" And he said, "In fact, you shall see it with your eyes, but you shall not eat of it."
(2Ki 7:1-2 NKJV)

These people were buying doves dung and eating their children, that is how bad the famine was (read 2Ki 6) However they were given Hope that within a day prosperity was coming. Hope brings Joy. I'm certain some people laughed at the prophet. Unfortunately the lead comedian who mocked saw the fruit of the Word but did not partake of the promise. This is why no matter how outrages or unbelievable a declaration from the Lord may be don't mock or doubt. You may laugh in joy but don't mock in unbelief.

So it happened just as the man of God had spoken to the king, saying, "Two seahs of barley for a shekel, and a seah of fine flour for a shekel, shall be sold tomorrow about this time in the gate of Samaria." Then that officer had answered the man of God, and said, "Now look, if the LORD would make windows in heaven, could such a thing be?" And he had said, "In fact, you shall see it with your eyes, but you shall not

eat of it." And so it happened to him, for the people trampled him in the gate, and he died.
(2Ki 7:18-20 NKJV)

Sarah also laughed when she overhead the Lord telling Abraham that she would have a child. Out of fear she denied that she laughed. This is the Joy the Hope of the Lord brings. There is spontaneous Joy of the Spirit and the Joy that something good is coming. With the famine of Samaria probably those who believed the word of Elisha began rejoicing immediately.

One of them said, "Nine months from now I will come back, and your wife Sarah will have a son." Sarah was behind him, at the door of the tent, listening. Abraham and Sarah were very old, and Sarah had stopped having her monthly periods. So Sarah laughed to herself and said, "Now that I am old and worn out, can I still enjoy sex? And besides, my husband is old too."
(Gen 18:10-12 GNB)

Sarah had lost Hope but said shall I have the pleasure of intimacy with my husband? We can see that the promise of God gives Hope for pleasures to be restored. Abraham and Sarah went on and had a good time while making the promise of God come to pass; Isaac.

As the Lord brings Hope, joy is standing right there ready to rejoice in victory. There are many great things the Father promises us as His children. This Hope will restore your Joy.

By whom also we have access by faith into this grace wherein we stand, and rejoice in hope of the glory of God. (Rom 5:2 KJV)

Confession

I will rejoice in the promises of God. My Hope in the Word of God brings me Joy. I cannot be sorrowful because great things are promised to me in Jesus name. Amen

---

The Hope of God brings joy! People may laugh spontaneously not knowing why. The joy is a confirmation of the Spirit man. The mind may not receive it but the Spirit man does.

A person standing alone can be attacked and defeated, but two can stand back-to-back and conquer. Three are even better, for a triple-braided cord is not easily broken. (Ecc 4:12 NLT)

At the introduction to this book on Hope we defined Hope. We concluded that Hope is a bond that attaches us to the Word and promises of God. Hope is the link that keeps us patient and expectant for the fulfillment of God's promises. One of the Hebrew words often translated as Hope means a rope or chord.

H8615

תִּקְוָה

tiqvâh

tik-vaw'

From H6960; literally a *cord* (as an *attachment* (compare H6961)); figuratively *expectancy:* - expectation ([-ted]), hope, live, thing that I long for.

Re: Strong's dictionary

Our opening scripture reveals to us the power of a triple threaded chord. It is not easily broken. When three people or attributes are threaded together they are stronger. A single thread can be broken much easier than if three threads are woven together. Similarly we have Hope in the Lord as a strong divine rope. This rope has the promise of God on one end and believers on the other end. We are linked and tied to God's Word by Hope our divine rope. We just have to hold on to that rope.

Rahab the prostitute helped the Israelite spies by lowering them down by a rope. In return they vowed to spare Rahab and all that were in her house.

"We offer our own lives as a guarantee for your safety," the men agreed. "If you don't betray us, we will keep our promise when the LORD gives us the land." Then, since Rahab's house was built into the city wall, she let them down by a rope through the window. (Jos 2:14-15 NLT)

The spies told Rahab to let down the red rope as a sign by her window. Which I believe was the same rope she let them down to escape.

Before they left, the men told her, "We can guarantee your safety only if you leave this scarlet rope hanging from the window. And all your family members—your father, mother, brothers, and all your relatives—must be here inside the house.
(Jos 2:17-18 NLT)

A red rope symbolizing the blood of Christ! These spies received a way out thanks to Rahab and this rope. It was their link to safety in turn they left it with Rahab as a sign of promise. All Rahab had to do was keep this red rope hanging out of her window and whoever was in the house would not be killed. This is similar to the Passover the Israelites kept, by putting the blood of the lamb on their doors to be kept safe.

But they burned the city and all that was in it with fire. Only the silver and gold, and the vessels of bronze and iron, they put into the treasury of the house of the LORD. And Joshua spared Rahab the harlot, her father's household, and all that she had. So she dwells in Israel to this day, because she hid the messengers whom Joshua sent to spy out Jericho. (Jos 6:24-25 NKJV)

Rahab was not only saved and her family but she is also in the lineage of Jesus Christ. All because of her kindness and that she held on to Hope in the promise the spies gave her.

Paul was nearly killed in his early ministry days but was let down by a basket held by a rope. That was the trust Paul had for his future at that moment. He was in a basket with a rope being held by believers at the other end.

But he was told of their plan. Day and night they watched the city gates in order to kill him. But one night Saul's followers took him and let him down through an opening in the wall, lowering him in a basket. (Act 9:24-25 GNB)

In the Old Testament ropes were used to tie down sacrifices when being offered to the Lord. They were also used to tie up enemies. The most important was probably ropes to hold tents and dwelling places up. When we Hope in God we tied to His promises.

Look upon Zion, the city of our solemnities: thine eyes shall see Jerusalem a quiet habitation, a tabernacle *that* shall not be taken down; not one of the stakes thereof shall ever be removed, neither shall any of the cords thereof be broken.

(Isa 33:20 KJV)

Prayer

Father thank you for the Hope you have given me. I am bound to your Word and promises to me in Jesus Christ. Amen

---

We are linked and tied to God's Word by Hope our divine rope.

Hope Says It Will Be Done – Day 22

I am with you and will watch over you wherever you go, and I will bring you back to this land. I will not leave you until I have done what I have promised you." When Jacob awoke from his sleep, he thought, "Surely the LORD is in this place, and I was not aware of it." (Gen 28:15-16 NIV)

As we saw in the previous day Hope is our rope linking us to God's promise. Just imagine you are pulling a rope with the promise of God attached at the end of it. When you've fully pulled the rope you receive what was at the end of the rope. This is why Hope does not leave until the promise is fulfilled. Hope says I'm here with you until you receive what I have for you.

God is not like people, who lie; He is not a human who changes his mind. Whatever he promises, he does; He speaks, and it is done.
(Num 23:19 GNB)

As believers we just have to keep a hold of that rope. Don't let go of your Hope in God. Abraham held on, Isaac held on, Jacob held on and they all saw the fulfillment of God's Word over them. Jacob remembered the promise the Lord gave him at Bethel and praised God when it was fulfilled.

Then Jacob said, O God of my father Abraham, the God of my father Isaac, the Lord who said to me, Go back to your country and your family and I will be good to you: I am less than nothing in comparison with all your mercies and your faith to me your servant; for with only my stick in my hand I went across Jordan, and now I have become two armies. (Gen 32:9-10 BBE)

The Lord is always faithful. Hope is there to keep us until His Word is fulfilled. Once we receive a particular promise from God we no longer need to Hope for that promise. We rejoice and enjoy the promise.

For it was by hope that we were saved; but if we see what we hope for, then it is not really hope. For who of us hopes for something we see? (Rom 8:24 GNB)

Declaration

I declare that I will keep a hold of Hope in what God has said to me until it is fulfilled in Jesus name. Amen

---

The Lord is always faithful. Hope is there to keep us until His Word is fulfilled.

My brethren, count it all joy when ye fall into divers temptations; Knowing *this,* that the trying of your faith worketh patience. But let patience have *her* perfect work, that ye may be perfect and entire, wanting nothing.

(Jas 1:2-4 KJV)

The gifts and talents the Lord Jesus gives us are for a reason. The anointing He gives to each person is for a purpose. We all have our own race we have to run and respond to our call in the areas we are called. No matter how gifted or anointed someone may be, if their character is weak they can bring more harm than good to the work of God. A solid character is humble yet wise and firm. Your character is perfected through trials. To overcome any trial patience and Hope are vital.

Understand that growth and development as a child of God is not determined by natural years. Someone may have been an Evangelist for twenty years but avoided or rejected the character development trials the Lord gave them. As a result this will be an unpolished Evangelist, not because of the Lord's mistake but because of the impatience and pride of the Evangelist.

On the other hand there can be a young Evangelist who has been in ministry for two years but has not avoided the school of the Spirit the Lord put him through. This Evangelist although in natural years has less experience than the elder Evangelist has a developed character. The Lord does not want pre-mature births of His gifts to the world; this is where patience and Hope come in.

And I will bring the third part through the fire, and will refine them as silver is refined, and will try them as gold is tried: they shall call on my name, and I will hear them: I will say, It *is* my people: and they shall say, The LORD *is* my God.

(Zec 13:9 KJV)

The Lord tests the hearts of people. A well developed character is clearly seen. Do not skip the training of God and run with the gift and anointing alone. You must be perfected. Hope enables you to endure trials, be strengthened, taught, renewed and perfected.

The fining pot *is* for silver, and the furnace for gold: but the LORD trieth the hearts.

(Pro 17:3 KJV)

The Lord checks the heart of a person, whether they will Humble themselves and receive His guidance. Ministers of God are different some submit to this more than others, it will be seen in their character. We are not judges of the people of God but character clearly shows itself over time. A character perfected by the Holy Ghost will be seen as a vessel of honour in the Kingdom of God.

But in a great house there are not only vessels of gold and of silver, but also of wood and of earth; and some to honour, and some to dishonour. If a man therefore purge himself from these, he shall be a vessel unto honour, sanctified, and meet for the master's use, *and* prepared unto every good work.

(2Ti 2:20-21 KJV)

Allow the Holy Ghost to work on you. Let patience work. Let Hope work. These two will bring you through the trials of life and perfect you.

And not only *so*, but we glory in tribulations also: knowing that tribulation worketh patience; And patience, experience; and experience, hope: (Rom 5:3-4 KJV)

Regardless of what you may go through, Hope is with you till you get an answer. It is this Hope that will help perfect your character. In the end you will be the finished product your Father desired. Only accept the correction, training and guidance of the Holy Ghost.

But He knows the way that I take; When He has tested me, I shall come forth as gold. My foot has held fast to His steps; I have kept His way and not turned aside. I have not departed from the commandment of His lips; I have treasured the words of His mouth More than my necessary food. (Job 23:10-12 NKJV)

Prayer

Lord develop and perfect me for what you have called me to do. Let patience, Hope and experience work in me for your Glory in Jesus name. Amen

A Better Hope – Day 24

For the law made nothing perfect, but the bringing in of a better hope *did;* by the which we draw nigh unto God.

(Heb 7:19 KJV)

The law of Moses had the children of Levi (the Levites) to serve in the office of the priesthood. Under the Old Testament they were to intercede for the people before God. They would offer sacrifices on behalf of the people before the Lord. They had to offer sacrifices for their own sins before they did so for the people. This was the Hope the children of Israel held to. If the sacrifice was accepted the people were covered for a period.

Make pomegranates out of blue, purple, and scarlet yarn, and attach them to the hem of the robe, with gold bells between them. The gold bells and pomegranates are to alternate all the way around the hem. Aaron will wear this robe whenever he enters the Holy Place to minister to the LORD, and the bells will tinkle as he goes in and out of the LORD's presence. If he wears it, he will not die.

(Exo 28:33-35 NLT)

Aaron ministered in the Priest's office and had to wear the

priestly robe with bells on it so he would not die in the presence of the Lord. This was the Old Testament. The people had to Hope that their representative did not die in the presence of the Lord. If he failed they were in trouble. The better Hope now is not dependent upon an earthly priesthood but a heavenly one. Then it was dependent upon the blood of bulls and goats but not now.

For such a High Priest was fitting for us, who is holy, harmless, undefiled, separate from sinners, and has become higher than the heavens; who does not need daily, as those high priests, to offer up sacrifices, first for His own sins and then for the people's, for this He did once for all when He offered up Himself. (Heb 7:26-27 NKJV)

The New Testament brought a better Hope for all. We now have Jesus Christ who offered himself as a sacrifice. There is now no need to daily offer sacrifices for sin but simply to accept the sacrifice of Jesus Christ. Our Hope is in the blood of Jesus.

For this *is* the covenant that I will make with the house of Israel after those days, saith the Lord; I will put my laws into their mind, and write them in their hearts: and I will be to them a God, and they shall be to me a people: And they shall not teach every man his neighbour, and every man his brother, saying, Know the Lord: for all shall know me, from the least to the greatest. For I will be merciful to their unrighteousness, and their sins and their iniquities will I remember no more. (Heb 8:10-12 KJV)

This is the Hope that was given to us through Christ, to have God's laws in our minds and hearts, to know Him personally and have our sins forgotten. Once you are born again you receive this promise. This is the New Covenant that we partake in as believers. It is the better Hope we received and now live in by Faith.

Remember Hope is until the promise is received. Now once someone accepts the Gospel they receive the promise of this better Hope; a life of Grace and Mercy covered by the blood of Jesus.

Neither by the blood of goats and calves, but by his own blood he entered in once into the holy place, having obtained eternal redemption *for us.* (Heb 9:12 KJV)

Declaration

I declare that I have received the promise from the better Hope of Jesus Christ. I live by faith in Jesus Christ and His works not my own efforts. Amen

Our Hope is in the blood of Jesus.

Which *hope* we have as an anchor of the soul, both sure and stedfast, and which entereth into that within the veil; (Heb 6:19 KJV)

An anchor is used by ships to keep them from drifting and being moved by the winds and waves. The Word of God says that we have this Hope as an anchor to our soul. What is this anchor?

Whither the forerunner is for us entered, *even* Jesus, made an high priest for ever after the order of Melchisedec.
(Heb 6:20 KJV)

Our Hope is Jesus Christ our High Priest. What was the role of the High Priest? His role was to intercede for the people of God before the Lord. Jesus has an eternal priesthood and has offered the sacrifice of himself which does not just cover our sins but wipes them away. What does it mean if our sins are wiped away? It means that they don't need to be paid for any more because they are gone! You are made holy and fully righteous!

This is the agreement which I will make with them after those days, says the Lord; I will put my laws in their hearts, writing them in their minds; he said, And I will keep no more memory of their sins and of their evil-doings. Now where there is forgiveness of these, there is no more offering for sin.
(Heb 10:16-18 BBE)

There is great power in sins being forgiven. The High Priest in the Old Testament would only enter the Holiest of Holies once a year behind the veil. Now Jesus has entered once and for all who believe in Him into the Holiest of Holies. He has made it possible for all who believe in Christ to receive forgiveness and dwell in the very presence of God. This is what anchors our soul; it prevents us from being moved by the winds and waves of the trials of life. We have an anchor, a Hope, a promise that we are in the presence of God.

Let your way of life be without the love of money, and be content with such things as you have, for He has said, "Not at all will I leave you, not at all will I forsake you, never!"
(Heb 13:5 MKJV)

A ship is not moved when it drops its anchor. This is similar to a hand brake on a car; it prevents the car from rolling down a hill. As believers we just have to remain anchored in our Hope in God's promise of being with us always. There is no need to pray Lord be with me, He said He is with you always! We must keep hold of this by faith.

Those who trust in the LORD Are like Mount Zion, Which cannot be moved, but abides forever. As the mountains surround Jerusalem, So the LORD surrounds His people From this time forth and forever.
(Psa 125:1-2 NKJV)

A mountain is not easily moved and we can even say is immovable. This is how we as children of God are with our Hope in the Lord Jesus. We are immovable from Trust in the Lord. Come what may we have a promise that something good coming because we are anchored in Christ. Our Hope is firmly and deeply rooted in the power of God.

Declaration

I declare that Jesus Christ is my Hope and my eternal anchor. I will not be moved by anything because I am firmly grounded in the promises of God in Jesus name. Amen

---

The Word of God says that we have this Hope as an anchor to our soul. What is this anchor? Our Hope is Jesus Christ our High Priest.

"As for you also, Because of the blood of your covenant, I will set your prisoners free from the waterless pit. Return to the stronghold, You prisoners of hope. Even today I declare That I will restore double to you.
(Zec 9:11-12 NKJV)

The Lord often showed His might and greatness in war. In the battles Israel would fight, the hand of the Lord would be seen bringing them great victories. God made a covenant with Israel and promised to stick to it; to be their God. In our opening verse the Lord again made reference to His agreement with Israel and instructed them to return to the stronghold.

What is a stronghold? In times of war a stronghold is a territory that is seen as safe and under an army or nations control. Whether that territory is rightfully theirs or not but it is firmly under their control. It is a fort. The Lord says return to the stronghold, you prisoners of Hope. The stronghold is in His presence, under His shadow, abiding by His Word. In the natural back then it could be seen as Jerusalem. In the Spirit it is the Heavenly Jerusalem.

Nevertheless David took the strong hold of Zion: the same *is* **the city of David.** (2Sa 5:7 KJV)

But ye are come unto mount Sion, and unto the city of the living God, the heavenly Jerusalem, and to an innumerable company of angels, (Heb 12:22 KJV)

In the City of the Living God is where there is safety. The Lord says abide there as a prisoner of Hope. This is one of the few occasions where I believe it is good to be prisoner. A prisoner of Hope; Hallelujah! This means you are arrested by the promise of God. You are immovable. Praise the Lord. You are locked up by Trust in God and the only way you will be released is when the promise is realized.

As children of God this is what Hope in the Lord is comparable to; a prisoner. You are caged by His Word of promise, until it comes to pass. A prisoner serves a sentence until they have completed their sentence. As a believer when you are Hoping for something from the Lord you must remain locked on Hope till it comes to pass. Look at Abraham, he was a prisoner to the prophecy he had of a child. Have you received any prophecies or words from the Lord?
Remain in the stronghold as a prisoner of Hope. Be unmoved by what you may be told from the outside remain fixed and attached to God's promise to you.

Return to your fortress, O prisoners of hope; even now I announce that I will restore twice as much to you. (Zec 9:12 NIV)

There is also the truth that a child of God who is a prisoner has Hope. We saw Paul and many of the early Christians where prisoners for Christ. They were arrested for their Hope in God. This is another view of a prisoner of Hope. There is also for them the same promise of double restoration.

Paul, a prisoner of Jesus Christ, and Timothy our brother, to Philemon the beloved and fellow laborer, and to Apphia the beloved, and to Archippus our fellow soldier, and to the church in your house.

(Phm 1:1-2 MKJV)

The ultimate truth of being a prisoner of Hope is being someone who has been captured by the Word of promise. This makes you immovable and fully grounded on what the Lord Jesus has said to you.

That Christ may dwell in your hearts by faith; that ye, being rooted and grounded in love,

(Eph 3:17 KJV)

Declaration

I declare that I am a prisoner of Hope in the promises of God to me. I will remain imprisoned by Hope until I receive the fulfillment of what has been promised to me in Jesus name. Amen

---

A prisoner of Hope; Hallelujah! This means you are arrested by the promise of God.

And hope does not make us ashamed, because the love of God has been poured out in our hearts through the Holy Spirit given to us.
(Rom 5:5 MKJV)

Shame comes from disgrace and dishonour. Whenever someone does something embarrassing they feel ashamed. Jesus Christ is the grace of God that has been given to all believers. We have this confidence and Hope that the grace of God will always cover anything that can bring a disgrace to our lives. This is why as a believer you will not be ashamed because you know your sins have been forgiven and wiped away.

There was a time when some of you were just like that, but now your sins have been washed away, and you have been set apart for God. You have been made right with God because of what the Lord Jesus Christ and the Spirit of our God have done for you.
(1Co 6:11 NLT)

But if we walk in the light, as he is in the light, we have fellowship one with another, and the blood of Jesus Christ his Son cleanseth us from all sin.
(1Jn 1:7 KJV)

The Apostle Paul explained clearly that even though grace overcomes sin we do not continue sinning. Understand that all the wrong we may have done in the past was shameful, we should not even make mention of it. Rather we should be thankful of the gift of righteousness we have been given.

What shall we say then? Shall we continue in sin so that grace may abound? Let it not be! How shall we who died to sin live any longer in it?
(Rom 6:1-2 MKJV)

What fruit did you have then in those things of which you are now ashamed? For the end of those things is death. But now, being made free from sin, and having become slaves to God, you have your fruit to holiness, and the end everlasting life.
(Rom 6:21-22 MKJV)

It is this Hope that we are forgiven, accepted and righteous by the blood of Christ that gives us confidence. We can be bold and unashamed in the presence of the Lord. God has given us His Holy Spirit as a seal and confirmation of His love for us. Therefore you cannot be ashamed because you have been justified by Jesus Christ.

That we should be to the praise of his glory, who first trusted in Christ. In whom ye also *trusted,* after that ye heard the word of truth, the gospel of your salvation: in whom also after that ye believed, ye were sealed with that holy Spirit of promise, Which is the earnest of our inheritance until the redemption of the purchased possession, unto the praise of his glory.
(Eph 1:12-14 KJV)

Adam and Eve were ashamed and hid from God when they had knowledge of good and evil and saw their nakedness. Before this they were naked but not ashamed.

And they were both naked, the man and his wife, and were not ashamed. (Gen 2:25 KJV)

Hope makes us unashamed because we have God's love. Now you don't need to be ashamed when people bring up your past because your past has been forgiven. You can boldly come to your Father without shame because Christ has paid for all your wrong.

For we have not an high priest which cannot be touched with the feeling of our infirmities; but was in all points tempted like as *we are, yet* **without sin. Let us therefore come boldly unto the throne of grace, that we may obtain mercy, and find grace to help in time of need.** (Heb 4:15-16 KJV)

As the Scripture says, "Anyone who trusts in him will never be put to shame." (Rom 10:11 NIV)

Act

Live without shame in God's presence. If ever you make a mistake repent and get up again.

For more on this read Forty Days On Grace & Forty Days On Righteousness by Jason Pullen

> God has given us His Holy Spirit as a seal and confirmation of His love for us. Therefore you cannot be ashamed because you have been justified by Jesus Christ.

Expectations Kept By Hope – Day 28

Let not thine heart envy sinners: but *be thou* in the fear of the LORD all the day long. For surely there is an end; and thine expectation shall not be cut off.
(Pro 23:17-18 KJV)

Have you ever waited expectantly for something? Perhaps an event you were looking forward to on a certain date or a parcel due for delivery. Maybe you've been in the hospital waiting for a bay to be delivered or at the airport waiting for a relative who's been away for a while. All these are examples of when someone can be excited anticipating something. The promises of God are just like that. Hope is what keeps us linked to that arrival time or due date. There is no cancelation.

Rest in the LORD, and wait patiently for him: fret not thyself because of him who prospereth in his way, because of the man who bringeth wicked devices to pass. Cease from anger, and forsake wrath: fret not thyself in any wise to do evil. For evildoers shall be cut off: but those that wait upon the LORD, they shall inherit the earth.
(Psa 37:7-9 KJV)

Many believers become discouraged when they see wicked people seeming to make it in life. They grumble and complain to the Lord, saying they are living in wickedness but their lives are better than mine. They compare themselves with others and think their own situation is hopeless. They may say I've done more for God but this other believer is ahead of me in life.

Your words have been stout against me, saith the LORD. Yet ye say, What have we spoken *so much* **against thee? Ye have said, It** *is* **vain to serve God: and what profit** *is it* **that we have kept his ordinance, and that we have walked mournfully before the LORD of hosts? And now we call the proud happy; yea, they that work wickedness are set up; yea,** *they that* **tempt God are even delivered.**
(Mal 3:13-15 KJV)

Do not be caught up in these comparisons. Run your own race there is Hope for you. There is an end. That means the end of trouble shall surely come. The end of your waiting shall surely come. Keep your expectations with Hope. The bible says the wicked shall be cut off but those that wait on the Lord shall inherit the earth. Know that serving and trusting God is not vain. Always be expectant of receiving from your Father. In the above scripture the people who listened to the prophet Malachi were recorded. The Lord said there will be a clear difference between those who serve Him and those who do not.

Then those who feared the LORD spoke to one another, And the LORD listened and heard them; So a

book of remembrance was written before Him For those who fear the LORD And who meditate on His name. "They shall be Mine," says the LORD of hosts, "On the day that I make them My jewels. And I will spare them As a man spares his own son who serves him." Then you shall again discern Between the righteous and the wicked, Between one who serves God And one who does not serve Him.
(Mal 3:16-18 NKJV)

From the story of the rich man and Lazarus we can see that earthly riches are vain.(see Luke 16) Jesus even said layup treasures in Heaven where they do not decay. (see Mat 6) Jesus also said a man's life does not consist in the abundance of things he has. (see Luk 12)

Eternal blessings are greater but there is still a promise of receiving a blessed, rich, glorious life here in this life. Peter asked Jesus what they would receive after giving up everything to follow Him. Jesus promised they would receive one hundred fold in this life. Therefore do not look at others but be expectant that you will see God's faithfulness in your life. Be unmoved as a prisoner of Hope that your life will testify of God's goodness.

And he said unto them, Verily I say unto you, There is no man that hath left house, or parents, or brethren, or wife, or children, for the kingdom of God's sake, Who shall not receive manifold more in this present time, and in the world to come life everlasting.
(Luk 18:29-30 KJV)

Hope keeps you linked to the goodness of God. Trusting that God is who He says He is should keep you expecting blessing from Him. He rewards those who seek Him. Riches and honour come from Him. Stand on His promises and you will see them.

Both riches and honor come from You, And You reign over all. In Your hand is power and might; In Your hand it is to make great And to give strength to all. "Now therefore, our God, We thank You And praise Your glorious name.
(1Ch 29:12-13 NKJV)

But without faith *it is* impossible to please *him:* for he that cometh to God must believe that he is, and *that* he is a rewarder of them that diligently seek him.
(Heb 11:6 KJV)

Confession

I confess that the Hope of the Lord keeps my expectations high of an ever increasing life enjoying His goodness and Glory. In Jesus name Amen.

Know that serving and trusting God is not vain. Always be expectant of receiving from your Father.

If ye continue in the faith grounded and settled, and
be not moved away from the hope of the gospel,
which ye have heard, *and* which was preached to
every creature which is under heaven; whereof I Paul
am made a minister;

(Col 1:23 KJV)

The Gospel is the message of good news of victory
brought through the death and resurrection of Jesus
Christ. There are many promises which were fulfilled by
the crucifixion and resurrection of Jesus Christ. This is the
Hope every believer must stand on until it is fulfilled.
Divine health, peace, prosperity, dominion and power
through Jesus are a few examples.

That is why he is the one who mediates the new
covenant between God and people, so that all who
are invited can receive the eternal inheritance God has
promised them. For Christ died to set them free from
the penalty of the sins they had committed under that
first covenant.

(Heb 9:15 NLT)

Jesus did not die in vain but left an eternal inheritance
available. All of mankind has the Hope of Salvation but
they must receive Jesus Christ. This is the Will of God that
all will be saved but it is each individual's choice. Once
one has received Salvation as a child of God there is the
Hope that Jesus died for. Jesus became poor so a child of
God can be rich. Jesus was wiped on His back so a child

of God can live in health. These are some of the things that Jesus left as an inheritance for believers. Our inheritance in Christ is what we must grab a hold of. Up until we see the manifestation of all this we keep the Hope of the Gospel for them to be fulfilled.

Now when someone dies and leaves a will, no one gets anything until it is proved that the person who wrote the will is dead. The will goes into effect only after the death of the person who wrote it. While the person is still alive, no one can use the will to get any of the things promised to them.
(Heb 9:16-17 NLT)

Jesus died and His Will is now in effect. The entire Will of Jesus Christ is the Hope of the world and of all born again Christians. Born again Christians however, have the right to claim and access everything that Jesus left for them as an inheritance. All of creation; animals, nature and so on are waiting for the Hope of the Gospel. They are waiting for the sons of God to take over and rule as Jesus desires.

The creation waits in eager expectation for the sons of God to be revealed. For the creation was subjected to frustration, not by its own choice, but by the will of the one who subjected it, in hope that the creation itself will be liberated from its bondage to decay and brought into the glorious freedom of the children of God. (Rom 8:19-21 NIV)

Up until we see the Church of Jesus Christ reigning as mature sons in Glory on earth we wait in Hope. God has declared that the whole earth will be filled with the knowledge of the Glory of the Lord. All people will know Him from the least to the greatest. This is what we stand to see.

For the earth will be filled With the knowledge of the glory of the LORD, As the waters cover the sea. (Hab 2:14 NKJV)

Declaration

I declare that I will stand in the Hope of the Gospel of Jesus Christ for my life and all of creation in Jesus name. Amen

---

Jesus died and His Will is now in effect. The entire Will of Jesus Christ is the Hope of the world and of all born again Christians.

The Hope Of His Calling ~ Day 30

That the God of our Lord Jesus Christ, the Father of glory, may give to you the spirit of wisdom and revelation in the knowledge of Him, the eyes of your understanding being enlightened; that you may know what is the hope of His calling, what are the riches of the glory of His inheritance in the saints,
(Eph 1:17-18 NKJV)

There is a reason God has called you. Every believer in Jesus Christ is called for a purpose. The Lord has entrusted believers with His authority and the preaching of the Gospel. The Hope of our call is directly connected to the Hope of the Gospel. We have a role to play and potential to reach in our walk with the Lord.

But as we have been approved by God to be entrusted with the gospel, even so we speak, not as pleasing men, but God who tests our hearts. For neither at any time did we use flattering words, as you know, nor a cloak for covetousness; God is witness.
(1Th 2:4-5 NKJV)

It is a great honour to be called by the Lord for a specific purpose. There is a Hope attached to your calling. There are people and situations that are dependent on Christians fulfilling their call from God. It is our duty as believers to pursue and obey what the Lord asks us to do with diligence. Not to abuse any authority given to us but to be faithful to the call. You never know who or what situation is Hoping on you doing what God called you to do. The Gentiles did not know but their Hope of hearing the Gospel was firmly attached to the Hope of Apostle Paul's call. If Paul did not obey his call many gentiles would be lost and we may not have had all his letters which make up the majority of the New Testament. Everyone's call matters.

Yet I considered it necessary to send to you Epaphroditus, my brother, fellow worker, and fellow soldier, but your messenger and the one who ministered to my need;
(Php 2:25 NKJV)

This brother Paul made mention of was walking in His call and was a comfort and provider to Paul. The Apostle Paul no doubt had a certain Hope that he (Epaphroditus) would continue walking in his call. This enabled Paul to carry out his ministry.

The Lord has a plan for all believers. At times believers do not even get into the second stage of their calling. You must understand there are levels to your call. The Lord desires for you to reach your full potential and the highest level He called you to. This is dependent on your faithfulness.

"Therefore you also be ready, for the Son of Man is coming at an hour you do not expect. "Who then is a faithful and wise servant, whom his master made ruler over his household, to give them food in due season? "Blessed is that servant whom his master, when he comes, will find so doing.
(Mat 24:44-46 NKJV)

The call of God on your life is connected to the Salvation of souls and their lives. Paul often told believers that they were his joy and crown. This is the Hope of your calling; the lives that you will impact. The fruit that you bear also gives you Hope. When you change a life, you have Hope that this person will turn and be a blessing to you. We are expectant that we will see fruit from responding to what Jesus asks us to do.

For what *is* our hope, or joy, or crown of rejoicing? *Are* not even ye in the presence of our Lord Jesus Christ at his coming? For ye are our glory and joy. (1Th 2:19-20 KJV)

Prayer

My Father help me to fulfill all that you have called me to do. I know that you are my strength and source in all things. Let everything in me give glory to you in Jesus name. Amen

---

The Lord desires for you to reach your full potential and the highest level He called you to. This is dependent on your faithfulness.

For it is written in the law of Moses, Thou shalt not muzzle the mouth of the ox that treadeth out the corn. Doth God take care for oxen? Or saith he *it* altogether for our sakes? For our sakes, no doubt, *this* is written: that he that ploweth should plow in hope; and that he that thresheth in hope should be partaker of his hope.

(1Co 9:9-10 KJV)

This wonderful theme scripture is taken from a portion where the Holy Spirit explains the right of ministers to receive financial and material support from the Saints. With an emphasis on not abusing this right and so hinder the Gospel. The point I want to take here is that anyone who ploughs (works for the Lord) must do so in Hope. Anyone who labours in the Gospel must do so with the Hope of a reward. This applies to all of life. Whatever you sow or put effort into especially the things of God you must do with Hope that you will harvest something good.

Whoever watches the wind will not plant; whoever looks at the clouds will not reap. As you do not know the path of the wind, or how the body is formed in a mother's womb, so you cannot understand the work of God, the Maker of all things.

(Ecc 11:4-5 NIV)

Unfortunately some believers will not give towards the Gospel or ministers or put much time in the things of God. This is because they have limited Hope in seeing a return. It is sad that some Saints would rather put money in several investments and spend much time in matters other than the Gospel. People may give all the reasons why they are limited in giving or the work in the Gospel. The main reason is that they are like that farmer who has no Hope; they wait for all conditions to be right and sure before stepping out. That is a faithless approach. Without faith someone cannot sow in Hope. We must trust God and realize we are not in control of all things. Hope is dependent on unseen things.

Sow your seed in the morning, and at evening let not your hands be idle, for you do not know which will succeed, whether this or that, or whether both will do equally well.
(Ecc 11:6 NIV)

A successful farmer plants and does not wait for perfect conditions. This is the way a believer should live. Give and work for the Kingdom, you don't know when your harvest will come. But you must plough in Hope. You must serve and give to the work of the Lord with Hope that you will see the blessings.

But this I say: He who sows sparingly will also reap sparingly, and he who sows bountifully will also reap bountifully.
(2Co 9:6 NKJV)

Anyone who sows sparingly is not doing so in Hope. One who gives their all to the things of God including money and resources is sowing in Hope. When someone does this they provoke the Lord to respond to His Word and show His faithfulness. The Lord keeps His Word; that whatever we give will be given back to us. How difficult is it to Hope in God who cannot lie?

Give, and it shall be given unto you; good measure, pressed down, and shaken together, and running over, shall men give into your bosom. For with the same measure that ye mete withal it shall be measured to you again.
(Luk 6:38 KJV)

Act

Plow in faith and hope.

> A successful farmer plants and does not wait for perfect conditions. This is the way a believer should live. Give and work for the Kingdom, you don't know when your harvest will come. But you must plough in Hope.

And we know that all things work together for good
to them that love God, to them who are the called
according to *his* purpose.
(Rom 8:28 KJV)

In life many things can happen, some designed by God,
some attacks by the devil and others by people's
decisions. It is important to note that not everything that
happens was destined by the Lord. God has a plan and
the devil has plan of destruction. People also have choice.
When all these come together you will find where you
are in life. The confidence and Hope we have as children
of God is that whatever has taken place in our lives God
can turn it around for good.

And we are conscious that all things are working
together for good to those who have love for God,
and have been marked out by his purpose.
(Rom 8:28 BBE)

Those who love God and are called according to His
purpose will see God working every situation for good.
This means that regardless of the attacks of the enemy or
foolish choices of people, the Lord is still able to get His
people back on track. The Lord Jesus is a wise master
builder and is able to restore and repair destinies.

And *they that shall be* of thee shall build the old waste
places: thou shalt raise up the foundations of many
generations; and thou shalt be called, The repairer of

the breach, The restorer of paths to dwell in.
(Isa 58:12 KJV)

We have this Hope that God will turn any life event around for our good. In ignorance some Christians accept anything in their life and say, all things will work together for my good. This is ignorance and a misunderstanding of the Word of God. As a believer you must use your authority to keep things in line with God's purpose for your life. Additionally you must make decisions led by the Holy Ghost. Never accept anything and say it is well, God will turn it for good. He has given you authority and the Holy Ghost to guide you.

"Behold, I give you the authority to trample on serpents and scorpions, and over all the power of the enemy, and nothing shall by any means hurt you.
(Luk 10:19 NKJV)

Having done your part, remain standing. In the Kingdom of God we are to do what the Lord tells us and remain standing. We stand in faith and wait in Hope for the fulfillment of His word to us. Our Father does His part and causes things to come together for our good and His purpose. We cannot do the Lord's part, we remain standing.

Wherefore take unto you the whole armour of God, that ye may be able to withstand in the evil day, and having done all, to stand.
(Eph 6:13 KJV)

After having done your part wait on the Lord. As you have learnt from earlier in this book, Hope enables you to wait. Jesus Christ is the creator of all things; He created you for His Glory. Rest in Hope that what He started with you, He will complete.

Being confident of this very thing, that he which hath begun a good work in you will perform *it* until the day of Jesus Christ:

(Php 1:6 KJV)

Declaration

I declare that I will follow the leading of the Holy Ghost and use my authority in the name of Jesus to do what is required of me. I am confident that my Heavenly Father will cause all things to work together for good in Jesus name. Amen

---

The confidence and Hope we have as children of God is that whatever has taken place in our lives God can turn it around for good.

Give Reasons For Your Hope – Day 33

But sanctify the Lord God in your hearts: and *be* ready always to *give* an answer to every man that asketh you a reason of the hope that is in you with meekness and fear:

(1Pe 3:15 KJV)

All born again Christians are representatives of the Kingdom of God. A citizen of a country is able to explain to a foreigner about life in their country. In like manner a child of God is a citizen of the Kingdom of God and should be able to speak of the Kingdom to unbelievers. Every nation has policies, plans and Hope for their future. As a child of God you must know; what is the Hope for every believer in God's Kingdom. You must be knowledgeable of the word of truth.

Preach the word; be instant in season, out of season; reprove, rebuke, exhort with all longsuffering and doctrine.

(2Ti 4:2 KJV)

Someone may say I'm not a preacher; I'm not called in that area. As a child of God you are a citizen of the Kingdom and must always be ready to give a word on why you trust in Jesus. The Saints of God have a work of service to the unsaved. You should be able to tell an unbeliever why they should want to be born again and a citizen in the Kingdom of God. Even world history confirms the events that took place at the crucifixion of Jesus. Current events too with numerous miracles and testimonies confirm the power of the Kingdom of God. The signs, miracles are wonders are just a way to attract someone to the love of King Jesus. Always be ready to testify of the Love of God.

His intention was the perfecting and the full equipping of the saints (His consecrated people), [that they should do] the work of ministering toward building up Christ's body (the church),
(Eph 4:12 AMP)

The Hope of Salvation is where to start with an unbeliever (we covered this on day 7). As a Christian you must know how to lead someone to Jesus Christ. This is done by leading them in the Salvation prayer (see the beginning of this book). Not everyone however will just pray along, they want to know why. This is when by the wisdom of God you must reveal why you have such Hope in God. Your personal testimony confirmed with scriptures is best. Have no fear the Lord Jesus will speak through you.

For it won't be you doing the talking—it will be the Spirit of your Father speaking through you.
(Mat 10:20 NLT)

An opportunity to represent the Kingdom in front of an audience can come at any time. As a believer there is the Hope of your call, lives will be dependent on you representing Christ well. Have no fear but always be expectant to speak on behalf of the Kingdom. The Holy Ghost will speak through you. Every child of God has a role to play in winning the lost. The Lord can use you in your own unique way, with your gifts to win souls. Do the work of an evangelist.

If any man speak, *let him speak* as the oracles of God; if any man minister, *let him do it* as of the ability which God giveth: that God in all things may be glorified through Jesus Christ, to whom be praise and dominion for ever and ever. Amen.
(1Pe 4:11 KJV)

There is always a reward for representing the Kingdom and winning souls. Remember as you take every opportunity to give a reason of your Hope in Christ you are ploughing. You are sowing and working in the vineyard of God.

But watch thou in all things, endure afflictions, do the work of an evangelist, make full proof of thy ministry.
(2Ti 4:5 KJV)

The fruit of the righteous is a tree of life, And he who wins souls is wise.
(Pro 11:30 NKJV)

Act

Always be ready to represent the Kingdom of God and win souls.

Hope from the Scriptures – Day 34

For everything that was written in the past was
written to teach us, so that through endurance and the
encouragement of the Scriptures we might have hope.
(Rom 15:4 NIV)

Throughout the New Testament there are references
made to the Old Testament and the Prophets. Everything
that was written in the bible has a purpose and it is for
our benefit. Whenever the Apostle Paul by the Holy
Ghost brought about a revelation, he would quote the
Old Testament.

It is not just in prophetic insight that we receive from the
bible but also in life lessons. At this point I must highlight
that not everything that is written in the bible is the
Gospel. There is murder, adultery, fornication, idolatry,
jealousy, betrayal and a whole lot of wicked things
recorded in the bible. It is the good news of Grace and
Mercy by the Blood of Jesus that we live by. All the other
events are lessons for us to learn from.

All scripture *is* given by inspiration of God, and *is*
profitable for doctrine, for reproof, for correction, for
instruction in righteousness: That the man of God may
be perfect, throughly furnished unto all good works.
(2Ti 3:16-17 KJV)

We learn what happened to the children of Israel when they worshipped a golden calf. They gave glory to the gold of Egypt as their deliverer. This provoked God to wrath. We see how David was honoured for standing for the name of the Lord. We see how Abraham was troubled by trying to fulfill God's promise having Ishmael. We also see how the Lord fulfilled His word to Abraham without his help bringing Isaac. These are a few examples where we can take lessons from. There are many other inspirational stories of triumph, faith and Hope. All these should be an encouragement that God can do it again.

Brothers and sisters, follow the example of the prophets who spoke in the name of the Lord. They were patient when they suffered unjustly. We consider those who endure to be blessed. You have heard about Job's endurance. You saw that the Lord ended Job's suffering because the Lord is compassionate and merciful.

(Jas 5:10-11 GW)

Take time to study the events in the Word of God there are gems hidden everywhere. There is something revealed all the time. Ask the Holy Ghost to show you the secrets and He will. The entire bible in inspired by the Lord. The bible is a spiritual book and will come alive to you as you search through it.

Knowing this first, that no prophecy of the scripture is of any private interpretation. For the prophecy came not in old time by the will of man: but holy men of God spake *as they were* moved by the Holy Ghost.

(2Pe 1:20-21 KJV)

We will always hear a mention of Abraham when we touch on Faith. We will hear of Isaac when we study on God's promise and Hope. Jacob will always come up when we search the love of God in the word. Be encouraged and comforted by the scriptures. Know that God cannot lie and what He says is true. This should keep you confident and Hopeful.

So God has given us both his promise and his oath. These two things are unchangeable because it is impossible for God to lie. Therefore, we who have fled to him for refuge can take new courage, for we can hold on to his promise with confidence.

(Heb 6:18 NLT)

Prayer

Heavenly Father teach me and reveal your wisdom and love to me as I read the bible. Let your word come alive to me and comfort me in Jesus name. Amen

---

Be encouraged and comforted by the scriptures. Know that God cannot lie and what He says is true.

But Naomi replied, "Why should you go on with me? Can I still give birth to other sons who could grow up to be your husbands? No, my daughters, return to your parents' homes, for I am too old to marry again. And even if it were possible, and I were to get married tonight and bear sons, then what?
(Rth 1:11-12 NLT)

The events that took place in the lives of Naomi and Ruth testify of the goodness of God, the reason to Hope and Power of His restoration. We receive comfort from the scriptures and this is an amazing testimony that should ignite Hope in you. Naomi had left her homeland with her husband and sons because of famine. Her sons married foreigners Orpah and Naomi. Tragedy struck and Naomi lost her husband and two sons. She was now left with two widowed daughter in laws. Naomi told them to go back to their families but Ruth insisted to stay with her.

But Ruth replied, "Don't urge me to leave you or to turn back from you. Where you go I will go, and where you stay I will stay. **Your people will be my people and your God my God.** Where you die I will die, and there I will be buried. May the LORD deal with me, be it ever so severely, if anything but death separates you and me."
(Rth 1:16-17 NIV)

There was absolutely no reason for Ruth to expect to receive anything from her mother in law Naomi. The situation looked hopeless. This is why Naomi said go from me you cannot wait for me to try and have another son and wait for him to grow. Ruth decided to remain faithful to her mother in law. She had married into this family and was concerned about the wellbeing of her mother in law. Naomi returned home and her name meaning pleasant/delight was not being lived up to. Upon her return she asked to be called Mara meaning bitter to reflect her experience.

And she said unto them, Call me not Naomi, call me Mara: for the Almighty hath dealt very bitterly with me. I went out full, and the LORD hath brought me home again empty: why *then* call ye me Naomi, seeing the LORD hath testified against me, and the Almighty hath afflicted me?

(Rth 1:20-21 KJV)

Naomi thought like Job (who we covered early in this book on day 16) that her disaster was from God. No this was the enemy who attacked her family. Naomi was in a bitter situation and so was Ruth her daughter in law. It seemed the rest of their lives would be spent mourning and in regret of the past. Can you imagine in that day even now a husband represents the strength wealth and standing of a family. These were two widows who seemed helpless. However with the Lord there is always Hope, He is a husband to the widow and a father to the fatherless.

A father of the fatherless, and a judge of the widows, *is* God in his holy habitation.

(Psa 68:5 KJV)

Ruth continued being faithful to her mother in law even in a poor state. She had to glean; that is to pick up the left over's from the harvesters in the field. This was how the poor would survive. It seemed gleaning was the Hope for Naomi and Ruth, living off leftovers. But God!
There was what I call a 'God incidence' not a coincidence that took place. Ruth went and glean in a certain field that changed their lives! Ruth received great favour from the owner of the field such that her mother in law Naomi was amazed at what she brought home. Ruth was given what was like a great harvest rather than left over's from gleaning; that shocked her mother in law.

"So much!" Naomi exclaimed. "Where did you gather all this grain today? Where did you work? May the LORD bless the one who helped you!" So Ruth told her mother-in-law about the man in whose field she had worked. And she said, "The man I worked with today is named Boaz."
(Rth 2:19 NLT)

Ruth had no idea that her Hope was about to be fulfilled by the Lord. She just happened to glean in the field of her kinsmen redeemer. Under the law the brother or one closest to a widow's deceased husband had to take his deceased brother's wife as his own. This was the law of a kinsmen redeemer. If the closest refused the next closest would take the right.

"If brothers dwell together, and one of them dies and has no son, the widow of the dead man shall not be married to a stranger outside the family; her husband's brother shall go in to her, take her as his wife, and

perform the duty of a husband's brother to her.
(Deu 25:5 NKJV)

Naomi probably in her sorrow forgot about this possibility for her daughter in law Ruth. The day she gleaned in Boaz's field she remembered the law and that this man had an obligation to take her as his wife.

And Naomi said unto her daughter in law, Blessed *be* he of the LORD, who hath not left off his kindness to the living and to the dead. And Naomi said unto her, The man *is* near of kin unto us, one of our next kinsmen. (Rth 2:20 KJV)

Boaz was a mighty man of wealth respected and known in the city. There however was a relative closer to Naomi than him who had first option to marry Ruth. This man refused and gave Boaz the right. Boaz had already had his eye on Ruth and heard her story of tragedy and faithfulness to Naomi. His heart was already soft and gracious towards Ruth.
So the moment he realized he had an obligation to marry her he jumped. We can see the hand of the Lord in this entire story.

And Boaz said to the elders and all the people, "You are witnesses this day that I have bought all that was Elimelech's, and all that was Chilion's and Mahlon's, from the hand of Naomi. "Moreover, Ruth the Moabitess, the widow of Mahlon, I have acquired as my wife, to perpetuate the name of the dead through his inheritance, that the name of the dead may not be cut off from among his brethren and from his position

at the gate. You are witnesses this day."
(Rth 4:9-10 NKJV)

Two widows living in poverty found their lives restored to greater than before! There is always Hope with God, regardless of what attack the devil has thrown at you. The city rejoiced at this redemption and spoke words of blessing over the marriage and children of Boaz and Ruth. Ruth was a Moabite, a descendant of Lot a people born through incest. Boaz was a descendant of Abraham of the tribe of Judah. Abraham and Lot (Abraham's nephew) reunited.

Then the women said to Naomi, "Blessed be the LORD, who has not left you this day without a close relative; and may his name be famous in Israel! "And may he be to you a restorer of life and a nourisher of your old age; for your daughter-in-law, who loves you, who is better to you than seven sons, has borne him." (Rth 4:14-15 NKJV)

This was redemption for the Moabites who seemed to be cursed because they were a product of incest between Lot and his daughter. Their Hope was restored and all Gentiles for they married into Israel under the tribe of Judah. Hope was fulfilled. The firstborn son from Boaz and Ruth was Obed whose name means serving. Obed just so happens to be the father of Jesse and grandfather of King David. Praise the Lord he knows how to turn darkness to light.

Regardless of the situation you may find yourself in the Lord can cause you to meet with people who will change your life. There is always Hope when you trust in God. Ruth just said to Naomi your God will be my God and God proved His faithfulness to Ruth.

Confession

I confess that I will never be put to shame by Hoping in God. I will be a testimony of the miracle working power of God. Like Ruth any darkness I have experienced will be turned around to shine with the redeeming light of God. In Jesus name. Amen

---

Ruth just said to Naomi your God will be my God and God proved His faithfulness to Ruth.

Zechariah & Elizabeth's Hope ~ Day 36

During the time when Herod was king of Judea, there was a priest named Zechariah, who belonged to the priestly order of Abijah. His wife's name was Elizabeth; she also belonged to a priestly family. They both lived good lives in God's sight and obeyed fully all the Lord's laws and commands. They had no children because Elizabeth could not have any, and she and Zechariah were both very old.

(Luk 1:5-7 GNB)

It is never too late for God to show His Power. Zechariah and Elizabeth both descendants of the tribe of Levi, priests of God lived a righteous life but suffered by never having children. This was something they were not over as we see when Zechariah was met by the angel Gabriel. For the angel told him that his prayer had been answered.

But the angel said to him, "Do not be afraid, Zacharias, for your prayer is heard; and your wife Elizabeth will bear you a son, and you shall call his name John. "And you will have joy and gladness, and many will rejoice at his birth.

(Luk 1:13-14 NKJV)

Barrenness was and is still often seen as a curse. No children would mean no continuation of a family name and heritage. This is the same thing that got to Abraham and Naomi. The Lord however came through for both of them. The testimony of Zechariah and Elizabeth is the same but different. Let's understand the meaning of their names to get a clear picture of what the Lord was showing us here.

The name "Zachariah" means **memory of the Lord**

The name "Elisabeth" means **the oath, or fullness, of God**

Re: Hitchcock's dictionary of Bible names

This couple married and priests of God the husband; memory of God and the wife; oath/promise of God. The memory of God and His promise were barren. This was meaning there was at the time an unfulfilled promise of God. Even though Zechariah and Elizabeth continued faithfully serving God and where now old they still hoped in God. Perhaps they did not fully believe but they kept Hope in God.
Once again the Lord came through and shocked them by giving them a child and not just any child, John the Baptist who Jesus declared as the greatest person born of women. (Before the new dispensation)

Verily I say unto you, Among them that are born of women there hath not risen a greater than John the Baptist: notwithstanding he that is least in the kingdom of heaven is greater than he.
(Mat 11:11 KJV)

Jesus saying this no doubt brought about debate and anger among the people. I'm certain many thought how can he be greater than Abraham, Jacob, Moses, Elijah, Elisha and King David people who did wonders and rescued Israel miraculously. Everyone who believed Jesus was the Messiah despite their thoughts had to take those words that John was the greatest. Imagine his parents Zachariah and Elizabeth? Without a doubt they too took the word and thought God had blessed them beyond what they expected. What does John name mean?

The name "John" means ***the grace or mercy of the Lord***

Re: Hitchcock's dictionary of Bible names

The Lord brought His grace out of the memory of His promise. The promise of the Lord to us is His unfailing love seen in His grace and mercy towards us. John was seen as the greatest because he is the one who announced the arrival of the Messiah, God's Salvation. From this testimony we learn that God will always remember His promise to us and bring about His love through Salvation. He will save you with His promise to you in whatever area you need it. Remember the name Jesus means Salvation. The name Jesus is the name above all names. So this promise provides in every area you need.

Our part is only to believe what God tells us. Zechariah doubted and the angel Gabriel made him dumb until John was born.

Zechariah said to the angel, "How can I know this will happen? I'm an old man now, and my wife is also well along in years." Then the angel said, "I am Gabriel! I stand in the very presence of God. It was he who sent me to bring you this good news! And now, since you didn't believe what I said, you won't be able to speak until the child is born. For my words will certainly come true at the proper time." (Luk 1:18-20 NLT)

When the Lord gives His word of promise, our part is to believe the promise and not to question or act in doubt but in faith. Elizabeth his wife took the word and was blessed for nine months until John's birth. Her husband however had to endure being unable to speak until John was born. The miracle that brought back Zechariahs speech amazingly was when he wrote out the name of his son; John.

So it was, on the eighth day, that they came to circumcise the child; and they would have called him by the name of his father, Zacharias. His mother answered and said, "No; he shall be called John." But they said to her, "There is no one among your relatives who is called by this name." So they made signs to his father; what he would have him called. And he asked for a writing tablet, and wrote, saying, "His name is John." So they all marveled. Immediately his mouth was opened and his tongue loosed, and he spoke, praising God.
(Luk 1:59-64 NKJV)

Mary was told of how she would be a virgin mother. She did not understand this but simply said let it be to me according to the word of God. This is the right thing to do when God declares His promise over you. Those who doubt may not be as fortunate as Zechariah and see the promise fulfilled. The king's servant who doubted the word of Elisha saw the fulfillment of God's Word but did not benefit from it.

Elisha replied, "Hear this message from the LORD! This is what the LORD says: By this time tomorrow in the

markets of Samaria, five quarts of fine flour will cost only half an ounce of silver, and ten quarts of barley grain will cost only half an ounce of silver." The officer assisting the king said to the man of God, "That couldn't happen even if the LORD opened the windows of heaven!" But Elisha replied, "You will see it happen, but you won't be able to eat any of it!"
(2Ki 7:1-2 NLT)

God promised what seemed impossible even if miraculous power was involved. There was a severe famine in the land. This is why the king's servant in a way was saying even if the supernatural takes place this cannot happen. The twenty four hour miracle happened and he saw it but did not enjoy it.

So it happened just as the man of God had spoken to the king, saying, "Two seahs of barley for a shekel, and a seah of fine flour for a shekel, shall be sold tomorrow about this time in the gate of Samaria." Then that officer had answered the man of God, and said, "Now look, if the LORD would make windows in heaven, could such a thing be?" And he had said, "In fact, you shall see it with your eyes, but you shall not eat of it." And so it happened to him, for the people trampled him in the gate, and he died.
(2Ki 7:18-20 NKJV)

Do not be faithless and unbelieving for GOD REMEMBERS HIS PROMISE OF LOVE TO YOU. Believe that anything is possible. God specializes in showing His power in the most unexpected ways under the most difficult situations. Let God be God simply believe in His Word and enjoy its fulfillment.

For with God nothing shall be impossible. And Mary said, Behold the handmaid of the Lord; be it unto me according to thy word. And the angel departed from her.
(Luk 1:37-38 KJV)

Prayer

Father I believe that you remember your promise of love towards me. I will always be expectant of seeing your faithfulness and miraculous working power because of this. I say like Mary; be it unto me according to your Word in Jesus name. Amen

God specializes in showing His power in the most unexpected ways under the most difficult situations.

Blessed *be* the God and Father of our Lord Jesus Christ, which according to his abundant mercy hath begotten us again unto a lively hope by the resurrection of Jesus Christ from the dead, To an inheritance incorruptible, and undefiled, and that fadeth not away, reserved in heaven for you,

(1Pe 1:3-4 KJV)

When something is dead there is no life in it. This may seem obvious to you but let's understand the relevance of this statement in Christianity versus religions and other belief systems. Every other leader or representative of a religion or faith died and is still dead! Therefore their Hope is dead. Jesus Christ is alive and therefore our Hope is alive.

If there is no resurrection of the dead, then not even Christ has been raised. And if Christ has not been raised, our preaching is useless and so is your faith.

(1Co 15:13-14 NIV)

The resurrection of Jesus Christ is what gives us Hope. We have a living Hope not a dead Hope which would be hopelessness. Faith is the substance of things Hoped for. We need to know that what we Hope for is genuine and true. This is what makes our faith genuine and true. A lot of people have Hope in a lie so ultimately their faith is a lie too.

Jesus Christ did a lot of talking on earth which upset the world and religious people to the point that they plotted and killed Him. They were not satisfied with killing Jesus but wanted to prove that all Christians had no Hope and that Jesus was a liar. Jesus made it clear that He would rise from the dead after three days. This was something His enemies were determined to stop at all costs because they knew it would prove truth.

The next day, which was the day of worship, the chief priests and Pharisees gathered together and went to Pilate. They said, "Sir, we remember how that deceiver said while he was still alive, 'After three days I will be brought back to life.' Therefore, give the order to make the tomb secure until the third day. Otherwise, his disciples may steal him and say to the people, 'He has been brought back to life.' Then the last deception will be worse than the first."
(Mat 27:62-64 GW)

They approached Pilate to guard the tomb. They did not want an empty tomb (grave). They knew it could ignite Hope in all people not just those who believed in Jesus when He was alive but in unbelievers too. To prevent Hope from remaining alive they posted soldiers to guard the tomb (grave).

Pilate told them, "You have the soldiers you want for guard duty. Go and make the tomb as secure as you know how." So they went to secure the tomb. They placed a seal on the stone and posted the soldiers on guard duty.
(Mat 27:65-66 GW)

The number of soldiers according to historians was no less than sixteen Roman soldiers and they probably were Jewish Temple guards there as well. The tomb (grave) was sealed with the Roman seal and the punishment was death for breaking the seal. There were also strict rules for the soldiers on guard; they faced the penalty of death if the 'prisoner' escaped or even if any of them fell asleep on duty.

Historians also tell us the entrance to the tomb was on a slope. This downhill made the boulder used to seal the tomb even heavier because of gravity. All this was done to prevent what the enemies of Jesus did not want to happen; the resurrection of Jesus Christ.

With the Roman Empire, the Jewish leaders and the devil and his demons satisfied that everything was done to prevent the resurrection they were at peace. However they were soon bitterly disappointed when all this failed. These leaders were met by trembling guards who left their duty to report what they saw. Now these were not wimps but men of war who were fearless and trained to stick to their orders till death. However they went to report what happened even though they knew they could be killed. No doubt the Roman and Jewish leaders were overcome by the genuine fear in the specialist guards and their willingness to risk death to report the matter.

And behold, there was a great earthquake; for an angel of the Lord descended from heaven, and came and rolled back the stone from the door, and sat on it. His countenance was like lightning, and his clothing as white as snow. And the guards shook for fear of him,

and became like dead men.
(Mat 28:2-4 NKJV)

As the women were on their way into the city, some
of the men who had been guarding the tomb went to
the leading priests and told them what had happened.
A meeting of all the religious leaders was called, and
they decided to bribe the soldiers. They told the
soldiers, "You must say, 'Jesus' disciples came during
the night while we were sleeping, and they stole his
body.' If the governor hears about it, we'll stand up
for you and everything will be all right." So the guards
accepted the bribe and said what they were told to
say. Their story spread widely among the Jews, and
they still tell it today.
(Mat 28:11-15 NLT)

We have a lively Hope, Jesus Christ is alive. As it was then
so it is now. The enemies of Jesus will spend a fortune
and use all their resources and lies to try and hide the
truth that Jesus is God and alive and well. Jesus did not
return to say; I told you so, to His enemies. He appeared
to His disciples and they were assured that their Hope is
alive and kept running. As a child of God, know that you
are trusting in the living God who will never disappoint
you. The enemies of Jesus feared for the resurrection
which they said would be a greater lie. We know that the
resurrection in fact is the greater truth!

Whom God hath raised up, having loosed the pains of
death: because it was not possible that he should be
holden of it.
(Act 2:24 KJV)

This *is* a faithful saying and worthy of all acceptation. For therefore we both labour and suffer reproach, because we trust in the living God, who is the Saviour of all men, specially of those that believe.
(1Ti 4:9-10 KJV)

Declaration

I declare that my Hope is alive for my saviour rose from the dead and is alive. I will not trust uncertain hopeless dead things but in Jesus Christ my living God. Amen

---

Every other leader or representative of a religion or faith died and is still dead! Therefore their Hope is dead. Jesus Christ is alive and therefore our Hope is alive.

Re: Historical facts on the burial of Jesus
https://www.blueletterbible.org/faq/don_stewart/don_stewart_247.cfm
https://bibleview.org/en/bible/easter/soldiers/

Blessed Hope - Day 38

Looking for that blessed hope, and the glorious
appearing of the great God and our Saviour Jesus
Christ; Who gave himself for us, that he might redeem
us from all iniquity, and purify unto himself a peculiar
people, zealous of good works.
(Tit 2:13-14 KJV)

Glory to God, we have a Blessed Hope. What is this
Blessed Hope? It is the appearing of our God and our
Saviour Jesus Christ. The word of God assures us of this
Hope; that Jesus Christ will come again with all those
who died in Christ. What is commonly believed as His
second coming.

We are telling you what the Lord taught. We who are
still alive when the Lord comes will not go into his
kingdom ahead of those who have already died. The
Lord will come from heaven with a command, with
the voice of the archangel, and with the trumpet call
of God. First, the dead who believed in Christ will
come back to life.
(1Th 4:15-16 GW)

So at this event believers who died in Christ will come
with Jesus. This is our Blessed Hope as the children of
God; the return of Jesus Christ. This is our Holy and
sacred trust for our eternal future the coming of Christ.
This event will happen but it is important to note that one
does not have to wait to see Jesus. The Blessed Hope is
the appearing of Jesus not just His coming with the dead

in Christ. It is the appearing of God and Jesus our Lord. The grace of God is Jesus Christ and He reveals Himself to everyone. Through grace He gives everyone an opportunity to know Him, a person must then decide from their heart to accept Jesus or not.

For the grace of God that bringeth salvation hath appeared to all men,
(Tit 2:11 KJV)

The grace of God appearing to all men however is not the Blessed Hope which we are speaking of here. The Blessed Hope is the actual appearing of Jesus Christ on His return and even before then. Now you may say what do you mean His appearing before His return with the Saints? Jesus has already appeared to people after He rose from the dead and ascended into heaven.

And as he journeyed, he came near Damascus: and suddenly there shined round about him a light from heaven: And he fell to the earth, and heard a voice saying unto him, Saul, Saul, why persecutest thou me? And he said, Who art thou, Lord? And the Lord said, I am Jesus whom thou persecutest: *it is* **hard for thee to kick against the pricks. And he trembling and astonished said, Lord, what wilt thou have me to do? And the Lord** *said* **unto him, Arise, and go into the city, and it shall be told thee what thou must do. And the men which journeyed with him stood speechless, hearing a voice, but seeing no man.**
(Act 9:3-7 KJV)

Jesus appeared to Saul after He had ascended into heaven. The appearing of Jesus is not limited to His promised return. The example above is of an occurrence of the appearance of Jesus after His ascension. However there have been many accounts of Jesus appearing to people since then. This is something as children of God we should be expectant of. It is a Blessed Hope to see your saviour. You do not need to die to see Jesus, He can appear to you.

And as it is appointed unto men once to die, but after this the judgment: So Christ was once offered to bear the sins of many; and unto them that look for him shall he appear the second time without sin unto salvation.
(Heb 9:27-28 KJV)

The above scripture verse twenty eight is an explanation of verse twenty seven. Jesus Christ died and took the judgment for man. Now those who believe and seek for Him will see His appearance. This is our Blessed Hope to see Jesus in our lives. Not just to see His power and love at work but even to see Him in person.

Henceforth there is laid up for me a crown of righteousness, which the Lord, the righteous judge, shall give me at that day: and not to me only, but unto all them also that love his appearing.
(2Ti 4:8 KJV)

We should have a strong desire to see the appearing of the Lord. Jesus can appear to whoever He pleases but I'm certain that He will appear to those who seek Him and desire His appearing. Understand this truth, even though our greater Hope is seeing the return of Jesus Christ with all those who died in Christ. This does not mean that you cannot see your Saviour before then. However keep a desire to see the power of God and His divine intervention in your life. He will show up for those who seek Him diligently.

And ye shall seek me, and find *me,* **when ye shall search for me with all your heart.**
(Jer 29:13 KJV)

Our role as believers in Christ is to remain expectant and Hopeful for the appearing of God. We must keep watch, which means to keep doing what we should as Christians in faith.

How is it that some people saw Jesus after His resurrection and others did not? Perhaps some of those Christians missed the news from the Apostles or were busy with something else. Where was Thomas that he missed the appearing of Jesus before the disciples? When we stop watching we may miss the appearance of Christ. So keep watch.

"Blessed are those servants whom the master, when he comes, will find watching. Assuredly, I say to you that he will gird himself and have them sit down to eat, and will come and serve them. "And if he should come in the second watch, or come in the third watch, and find them so, blessed are those servants.
(Luk 12:37-38 NKJV)

The devil and those in the world mock and say where, is this return of Jesus? They mock as if to say where is the Hope of these believers? They ridicule our Blessed Hope. The word of God however is clear that Jesus will come again. Believers will be received and blessed in the Kingdom but unbelievers will be condemned to hell.

First, I want to remind you that in the last days there will be scoffers who will laugh at the truth and do every evil thing they desire. This will be their argument: "Jesus promised to come back, did he? Then where is he? Why, as far back as anyone can remember, everything has remained exactly the same since the world was first created." They deliberately forget that God made the heavens by the word of his command, and he brought the earth up from the water and surrounded it with water. Then he used the water to destroy the world with a mighty flood. (2Pe 3:3-6 NLT)

Our direction and Hope with God is found in His Word. The Lord will not do anything against His Word. Whoever desires to know the truth of our faith should look to the word. Unbelievers will want some major sign but we are given His Word. For when the Lord rid the world of wickedness in the days of Noah no one knew what was coming except Noah. Noah had the Word of the Lord the others did not or did not believe the one with the Word.

"But as the days of Noah were, so also will the coming of the Son of Man be. "For as in the days before the flood, they were eating and drinking, marrying and giving in marriage, until the day that Noah entered the ark, "and did not know until the flood came and took them all away, so also will the coming of the Son of Man be.

(Mat 24:37-39 NKJV)

Declaration

I declare that I have a Blessed Hope; the appearing of my God and Saviour Jesus Christ. I will not be drawn away but continue in Faith for I love the appearing of Jesus. I declare that I am expectant of the appearing of Jesus even before His promised return. Amen

---

Glory to God, we have a Blessed Hope. What is this Blessed Hope? It is the appearing of our God and our Saviour Jesus Christ

---

Brothers and sisters, we don't want you to be ignorant about those who have died. We don't want you to grieve like other people who have no hope.
(1Th 4:13 GW)

It's important to know Our Heavenly Father does not kill (take) His children. It is the devil who comes to steal, kill and destroy. Regardless of how someone dies, whether it was in peaceful sleep after a long blessed life, death is still an enemy. This is why we have the Hope of the resurrection from the dead. God does not even rejoice in the death of the wicked! He desires life and Salvation.

As surely as I live, says the Sovereign LORD, I take no pleasure in the death of wicked people. I only want them to turn from their wicked ways so they can live. Turn! Turn from your wickedness, Opeople of Israel! Why should you die?
(Eze 33:11 NLT)

The last enemy *that* shall be destroyed *is* death.
(1Co 15:26 KJV)

Jesus did not go about striking people down or killing those who rejected Him. He taught that we should love our enemies and pray for those who persecute and use us. When Jesus was not received by some Samaritans; James and John thought it would be good for the destruction of that place. This must have been a serious rejection that the disciples thought they were worthy of death by fire.

And sent messengers before His face. And as they went, they entered a village of the Samaritans, to prepare for Him. But they did not receive Him, because His face was set for the journey to Jerusalem. And when His disciples James and John saw this, they said, "Lord, do You want us to command fire to come down from heaven and consume them, just as Elijah did?" But He turned and rebuked them, and said, "You do not know what manner of spirit you are of. "For the Son of Man did not come to destroy men's lives but to save them." And they went to another village.
(Luk 9:52-56 NKJV)

Jesus stood for life for His enemies. Why? So that they could have a chance to repent and enter the Kingdom of God. The Lord does not want to see the death of His enemies but their Salvation. This is why as believers we must stand in Hope of the resurrection of the dead. For Jesus came to give life, death entered because of sin. Sin came because of the devil. Jesus died to remove the power of sin and ultimately the power of death.

The sting of death is sin, and the strength of sin is the law. But thanks be to God, who gives us the victory through our Lord Jesus Christ.
(1Co 15:56-57 NKJV)

By faith we can raise the dead. Jesus even told us to raise the dead. God is for life. The main Hope of resurrection however is that of all those who have died in Christ.

Whether someone died a week ago or hundreds of years ago, there is the Hope that they will be raised back to life with an incorruptible body. This is all possible because Jesus rose from the dead; we have a Living Hope (See Day 37). If Jesus did not rise from the dead then we would have no Hope.

Now if Christ is preached that He has been raised from the dead, how do some among you say that there is no resurrection of the dead? But if there is no resurrection of the dead, then Christ is not risen. And if Christ is not risen, then our preaching is empty and your faith is also empty.
(1Co 15:12-14 NKJV)

Jesus rose from the dead and at that time all those Saints who died where raised after Him! They even appeared to people in the city.

Jesus, when he had cried again with a loud voice, yielded up the ghost. And, behold, the veil of the temple was rent in twain from the top to the bottom; and the earth did quake, and the rocks rent; And the graves were opened; and many bodies of the saints which slept arose, And came out of the graves after his resurrection, and went into the holy city, and appeared unto many.
(Mat 27:50-53 KJV)

Those Saints ascended with Jesus.

And when he had spoken these things, while they beheld, he was taken up; and a cloud received him out of their sight. (Act 1:9 KJV)

The cloud here is the people, the cloud of witnesses as Hebrews reveals to us.

Wherefore seeing we also are compassed about with so great a cloud of witnesses, let us lay aside every weight, and the sin which doth so easily beset *us,* and let us run with patience the race that is set before us, (Heb 12:1 KJV)

This is the same cloud (saints) that the bible says will return with Jesus at His return. This is when the dead in Christ will rise with their bodies. This is the Hope of the resurrection.

And then shall they see the Son of man coming in a cloud with power and great glory.
(Luk 21:27 KJV)

For the Lord himself shall descend from heaven with a shout, with the voice of the archangel, and with the trump of God: and the dead in Christ shall rise first: Then we which are alive *and* remain shall be caught up together with them in the clouds, to meet the Lord in the air: and so shall we ever be with the Lord. Wherefore comfort one another with these words.
(1Th 4:16-18 KJV)

At the return of Jesus Christ the dead will rise and their corrupted bodies (decayed) will become incorruptible and our mortal (liable to death) bodies will become immortal. This is our Hope as believers. When a Christian dies we should not mourn like those who have no Hope. This scripture above must be our comfort of Hope. There is no need to continue wailing as if you will never see a Saint who has died again.

At one time a believer in Christ who I knew and was close to died. We cried and my fellow believers cried too. But after some time I wondered why some continued wailing and mourning. I asked the Lord why am I not howling like these others is my heart hard or perhaps I wasn't as close to this Saint. The Lord Jesus said to me, no it is because you believe my word and they don't. He told me I believed the resurrection but others believed that was the end of life for this Saint. They were mourning as those who have no Hope.

Now also we would not have you ignorant, brethren, about those who fall asleep [in death], that you may not grieve [for them] as the rest do who have no hope [beyond the grave].

(1Th 4:13 AMP)

Grieving is prolonged sorrow. As Christians we do not mourn or grieve when a loved one dies. We may cry, feel sad but not for a continued period. As believers we are comforted by the Holy Ghost and by the Word of God. The Word of God and His Spirit gives strength and comfort not words saying sorry or seeking attention or self pity. Seeking for people to cry with you or feel sorry for you after losing a loved one will not comfort you. Only the comforter the Holy Ghost and His Word will comfort and bring you Joy.

I can tell you this directly from the Lord: We who are still living when the Lord returns will not rise to meet him ahead of those who are in their graves. For the Lord himself will come down from heaven with a commanding shout, with the call of the archangel, and with the trumpet call of God. First, all the Christians who have died will rise from their graves. Then, together with them, we who are still alive and remain on the earth will be caught up in the clouds to meet the Lord in the air and remain with him forever. So comfort and encourage each other with these words.
(1Th 4:15-18 NLT)

Confession

I confess that I have the Hope of resurrection because Jesus rose from the dead. I will not mourn or grieve as those with no Hope. I have Hope in Jesus and comfort from the Holy Ghost and His Word over every loved one who has passed on. I will likewise share this comfort to others in Jesus name. Amen

---

Seeking for people to cry with you or feel sorry for you after losing a loved one will not comfort you. Only the comforter the Holy Ghost and His Word will comfort and bring you Joy.

Christ The Hope Of Glory ~ Day 40

Even the mystery which hath been hid from ages and from generations, but now is made manifest to his saints: To whom God would make known what *is* the riches of the glory of this mystery among the Gentiles; which is Christ in you, the hope of glory:
(Col 1:26-27 KJV)

By now you should have a clear understanding of what Hope is. It is that great expectation we have for the fulfillment of God's Word. Christ in us is our firm expectation of Glory. Every born again believer has the seed of God; Christ in them. This seed has great potential this is why we have Hope. As we mature as believers we see the manifestation of the power and Glory of God in greater ways.

Now to Abraham and his seed were the promises made. He saith not, And to seeds, as of many; but as of one, And to thy seed, which is Christ.
(Gal 3:16 KJV)

This seed (Christ) is in us as our opening scripture states. Jesus always explained the Kingdom in parables and often spoke of three measures. This was to express the growth of believers in Christ, they are either immature (babies) semi mature or mature. That bears fruit thirty, sixty or hundredfold.

Anyone who has to drink milk is still a child, without any experience in the matter of right and wrong. Solid food, on the other hand, is for adults, who through

practice are able to distinguish between good and evil.
(Heb 5:13-14 GNB)

Every child needs to grow. The desire of every parent is to see their child grow into a mature and excellent man or woman. Milk is the basics of the Word of Faith and is for immature Christians. As you mature you are concerned with the greater glorious things in the Kingdom. This is the desire of God, the growth and perfection of His children the Saints.
Every tree after being planted needs to grow to bear fruit. Likewise believers have to grow to see fruit and Glory. Paul even spoke to believers in Galatia saying that his desire was to see Christ formed in them.

My little children, of whom I travail in birth again until Christ be formed in you,

(Gal 4:19 KJV)

When Christ is formed it means your appearance is like Christ, your speech and behavior is like Christ. This is a mature Christian one who is like Christ. At the time of receiving Christ we are made sons of God. However we must grow into mature sons. This is our Hope of Glory to be mature sons of God.

Beloved, now are we the sons of God, and it doth not yet appear what we shall be: but we know that, when he shall appear, we shall be like him; for we shall see him as he is. And every man that hath this hope in him purifieth himself, even as he is pure.

(1Jn 3:2-3 KJV)

At the appearing of Jesus Christ all believers will look like him. How does Jesus look? He is Glorious and perfect. We do not have to wait for the return of Christ but in this life we should mature and allow the Word of God and His Spirit to shape us into mature sons of God. This way we will walk with authority and power just like Peter and Paul did. A mature son of God knows who they are and is not driven by every teaching that is out there. They know the way of the Kingdom of God and walk in power.

Till we all come in the unity of the faith, and of the knowledge of the Son of God, unto a perfect man, unto the measure of the stature of the fulness of Christ: That we *henceforth* be no more children, tossed to and fro, and carried about with every wind of doctrine, by the sleight of men, *and* cunning craftiness, whereby they lie in wait to deceive; But speaking the truth in love, may grow up into him in all things, which is the head, *even* Christ: From whom the whole body fitly joined together and compacted by that which every joint supplieth, according to the effectual working in the measure of every part, maketh increase of the body unto the edifying of itself in love.

(Eph 4:13-16 KJV)

This is our Hope of Glory; a mature Church who knows who they are and walk in unity. Experts in any field will agree on the basics and know how things work. This is what mature citizens in God's Kingdom are like they agree on truth and know how the Kingdom works. Mature sons of God are the ones who will rule in power and Glory.

For I reckon that the sufferings of this present time *are* not worthy *to be compared* with the glory which shall be revealed in us. For the earnest expectation of the creature waiteth for the manifestation of the sons of God.
(Rom 8:18-19 KJV)

The word translated as sons above means mature sons. All of creation is waiting for the mature sons of God to be revealed. This I believe is what will bring redemption and Glory to the world. All of creation has Hope in the Saints maturing in Christ.

Everything God created looks forward to the time when his children will appear in their full and final glory.
(Rom 8:19 NIRV)

Prayer

Father thank you for giving me your life that is found in your son Jesus Christ. Let your Spirit and Word bring me to perfection and maturity that I will be a blessing to this world in Jesus name. Amen

Experts in any field will agree on the basics and know how things work. This is what mature citizens in God's Kingdom are like they agree on truth and know how the Kingdom works.

Conclusion

Anyone who has given their life to Jesus Christ has Hope. Hope our great expectation for the future is always there. We are rooted and anchored by the promises of God to us. Our Hope in God is a divine rope that keeps us tied to His word of promise. Until we receive whatever we are believing God for we are comforted and patient by Hope.

The bible says there is Hope for a tree that if it is cut down it will sprout again. There is always a reason to expect restoration of more than what was lost with God. Regardless of the darkness that has come upon someone there is always a day star that will arise. The light of God Jesus Chris will always bring light out of darkness.

We do not depend on man but trust in the Lord. Keeping trust in what God says will not lead to disappointment. No one that has Hope in God will ever be put to shame. So soak up everything that is in this book. Read over it and let the Spirit Word of God take root in you. Know what is yours and take it by faith.

Blessed *is* the man that trusteth in the LORD, and whose hope the LORD is. For he shall be as a tree planted by the waters, and *that* spreadeth out her roots by the river, and shall not see when heat cometh, but her leaf shall be green; and shall not be careful in the year of drought, neither shall cease from yielding fruit.
(Jer 17:7-8 KJV)

With Love & Blessings

Jason Pullen

Other Books by the Author

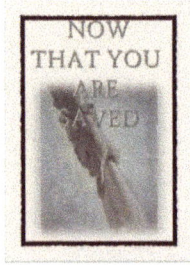

NOW THAT YOU ARE SAVED

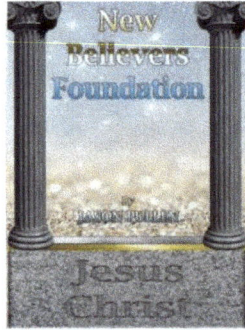

New Believers Foundation

JASON PULLEN

Jesus Christ

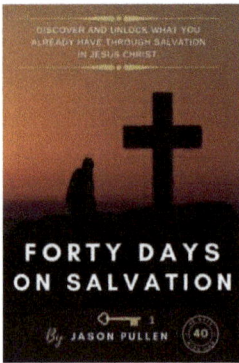

DISCOVER AND UNLOCK WHAT YOU ALREADY HAVE THROUGH SALVATION IN JESUS CHRIST.

FORTY DAYS ON SALVATION

By JASON PULLEN

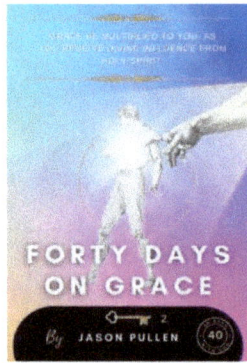

GRACE IS MULTIPLIED TO YOU AS YOU RECEIVE LIVING INFLUENCE FROM GOD IN CHRIST

FORTY DAYS ON GRACE

By JASON PULLEN

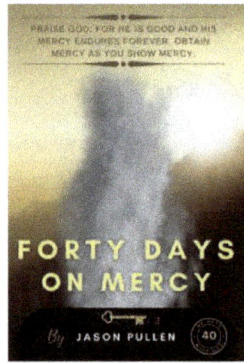

PRAISE GOD, FOR HE IS GOOD AND HIS MERCY ENDURES FOREVER. OBTAIN MERCY AS YOU SHOW MERCY.

FORTY DAYS ON MERCY

By JASON PULLEN

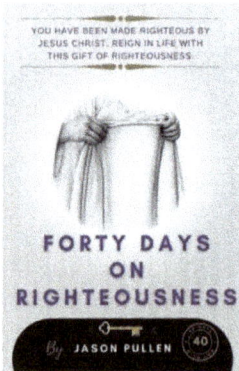

YOU HAVE BEEN MADE RIGHTEOUS BY JESUS CHRIST. REIGN IN LIFE WITH THIS GIFT OF RIGHTEOUSNESS.

FORTY DAYS ON RIGHTEOUSNESS

By JASON PULLEN

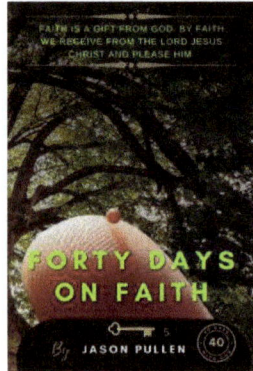

FAITH IS A GIFT FROM GOD. BY FAITH WE RECEIVE FROM THE LORD JESUS CHRIST AND PLEASE HIM

FORTY DAYS ON FAITH

By JASON PULLEN

www.ingramcontent.com/pod-product-compliance
Lightning Source LLC
Chambersburg PA
CBHW051839090426
42736CB00011B/1885